Through The Years......,,,

A Collection of E-mail Jokes, Random Thoughts and Other Funny Stuff

Gathered by Dr. Alan G. Greene

authorHOUSE™

1663 LIBERTY DRIVE, SUITE 200
BLOOMINGTON, INDIANA 47403
(800) 839-8640
WWW.AUTHORHOUSE.COM

First published by AuthorHouse 01/18/06

ISBN: 1-4208-6489-0 (sc)

Printed in the United States of America
Bloomington, Indiana

This book is printed on acid-free paper.

Dedicated to my wife Susan who puts up with my hogging the computer and to all those who enjoy this kind of thing, and want to continue it by forwarding stuff to their friends.

FOREWORD

Spam is an unfortunate part of today's technology that one is subjected to on a routine basis. But a more enjoyable reward of computerized technology is the exchange of humor passing through cyberspace. This passage can sometimes be a pain in the butt, but more frequently it is a delight and a looked forward to experience.

It has been said that the rapidity of transmission of jokes across the country can be an indication of the state of the economy. If business is good, the speed of jokes going from one coast to the other is very fast. But if the economy is saging, it taking longer. Be that as it may, I hope you enjoy the following thoughts and transmissions.

I want to thank the following for their e-mails and the daily enjoyment I've had from their transmissions: David Berger, Warren Mitofsky, Jane and Mitch Weingrad, Mark Matluck, Jules Schwartz, and Richard Ellis. (There are likely others involved, but I frequently can't tell the origins of the stories.)

A Third World dipolomat visiting the U.S. for the first time was being wined and dined by the State Department. The diplomat was not used to the salt in American food (French fries, cheeses, salami, anchovies etc.) and was constantly sending his manservant to fetch him a glass of water. Time and again, his servant would scamper off and return with a glass of water, but then came the time when he returned empty handed. "You son of an ugly camel, where is my water?" demanded the diplomat. "A thousand pardons, O Illustrious One," stammered the wretched servant.

"A man is sitting on the well!"

Results of a contest in which readers were asked to supply alternate meanings for various words. The following are some of the winning entries.

1.Coffee (n.) a person who is coughed upon

2.Flabbergasted (adj.) appalled over how much weight you have gained.

3. Abdicate (v.) to give up all hope of ever having a flat stomach.

4. Willy-nilly (adj.) impotent.

5. Negligent (adj.) describes a condition in which you absentmindedly answer the door in your nightie.

6. Lymph (v.) to walk with a lisp.

7. Gargoyle (n.) an olive-flavored mouthwash.

8. Flatulence (n.) the emergency vehicle that picks you up after you have been run over by a steamroller.

9. Balderdash (n.) a rapidly receding hairline

10. Testicle (n.) a humorous question on an exam.

11. Rectitude (n.) the formal, dignified demeanor assumed by a proctologist immediately before he examines you.

12. Oyster (n.) a person who sprinkles his conversation with Yiddish expressions.

13. Frisbetarianism (n.) the belief that, when you die, your soul goes up on the roof and gets stuck there.

14. Pokemon (n.) a Jamaican proctologist.

Things you can get away with saying only at Thanksgiving

1. I prefer breasts to legs.

2. Tying the legs together keeps the inside moist.

3. Smother the butter all over the breasts!!

4. If I don't undo my trousers, I'll burst.

5. I've never seen a better spread.

6. I'm in the mood for a little dark meat.

7. Are you ready for seconds yet?

8. It's a little dry, do you still want to eat it?

9. Just wait your turn, you'll get some.

10. Don't play with your meat.

11. Stuff it up between the legs as far as it will go.

12. Do you think you'll be able to handle all these people at once?

13. I didn't expect everyone to come at the same time!

14. You have a little bit on your chin.

15. How long will it take after you put it in?

16. You'll know it's ready when it pops up'

17. That's the biggest bird I've ever had!

18. I'm so full, I've been gobbling nuts all morning.

19. Wow, I didn't think I could handle all that and still want more.

Rather than getting married, then divorced. I've just decided to find a woman I don't like and give her my house.

Tried to pick up a girl in a bar. Asked her, "What's your sign." She said, "Do not enter."

My wife went shopping and bought an escalator. She'll buy anything that is marked 'DOWN'.

Came home and found all my clothes thrown out on the lawn. I asked my girlfriend, "What's happening?" She said, "I just found out you're a pedophile" I said, "That's an awfully big word for a 10 year old."

Three nuns were talking. One said, "I was going through Father Johnson's desk looking for something and I found a bunch of copies of Playboy and Penthouse and I threw them out". The second nun said, "I had to find something in Father O'Leary's desk and I found all these condoms, so I punched a hole in all of them". The third nun said, "Oh, s—t".

This fellow was a born executive, his father owned the company.

Q-What do you call a gay dentist?
A-A tooth fairy.

Travel is very educational. I can now say 'kaopectate' in 7 languages.

This guy in a bar says very loudly, "All lawyers are a—holes."
The man sitting next to him says, "I'll have to take issue with that and disagree with you."
The first guy says, "I'll bet you're a lawyer".
To which the man replies, "No, I'm an a—hole."

Q-What happens to lawyers when they take Viagra?
A-They get taller."

This monk enters a monastery where they are allowed to say only two words every ten years. At the end of the first 10 years he says, "Bed hard." 10 years later, he says "Food bad." 10 years later, he says, "I quit."

The head of the monastery says, "No wonder, you've been here 30 years and all you've done is bitch, bitch, bitch."

One woman in an assisted living facility has been playing cards with this other lady every day for a couple of years. One morning, very ashamedly, she says, "You'll have to forgive me, but I've forgotten your name. What is it?' The other woman thinks for a second and says, "How soon do you need to know?"

An elderly man is at the doctor's office for his yearly physical. The doctor, when he hears that the man is still sexually active, says, "I hope you use precautions." The old man answers, "I ain't senile, I use a phony name."

Two 90-year olds have sex. The man tells a friend, "If I knew she was a virgin, I would have been gentler." She tells a friend, "If I'd known the old geezer could do it, I would have taken off my panty hose."

There are two theories about arguing with women. Neither one works.

Q-Why did God invent man?
A-Because a vibrator can't mow the lawn.

Mother vampire to son, "Eat your breakfast before it clots."

Q-Why don't blind people sky-dive?
A-It scares the hell out of the dog.

"If at first you don't succeed, try, try again" is not a good motto for a sky-diver

Movie sequels nobody wants to see:

1)Commandments 11-20. Moses Strikes Back

2)Three Men and a Sheep

3)Rocky 10:Rocky Fights Irregularity

4)Police Academy IX:Beating a Dead Horse

5)Babe III:Side of Bacon

6)Showgirls 2001:A Silicon Odyssey

7)Eliminating Raoul

8)Home Alone: Under House Arrest

9)Dead Man Rotting

10)Driving Miss Daisy's Hearse

11)Pee Wee's Felonious Adventure

12)Lawrence of Bolivia

13)Kickboxer 3:Right In The Groin

14)Weekend At Bernie's:Starting To Reek

Q-What do you get when you cross the Atlantic Ocean with the Titanic?
A-About half way.

Knock-knock joke in N.Y.
Knock-knock
Who's there?
None of your God-damned business

Two guys go out for a walk with their dogs. One has a German Shepherd, the other has a Chihuahua The fellow with the German Shepherd suggests they stop in a bar for a drink. The other guy says they'll never let us into a bar with the dogs. The first guy says, "Put on your sun glasses and say they are seeing eye dogs." They come up to a bar and the guy with the German Shepherd goes in. The bartender stops him and says, "You can't come in here with that dog." To which he says, "This is my seeing-eye dog and he has to be with me at all times." The bartender says, "Okay, you can come in." The second guy comes in a few minutes later with his Chihuahua and the bartender stops him and says, "You can't come in here with that dog." He answers, "This is my seeing-eye dog and he must be with me at all times." The bartender says, "Give me a break, I've never seen a seeing-eye Chihuahua." And the man replies, "They gave me a Chihuahua?"

With all the warnings about sexually transmitted diseases, I thought phone sex would be safe. But, my luck, I got an ear infection.

I was in a bar in Vermont and the guy next to me was talking with a very gravelly voice and I asked him why he was talking that way. He said, "He was playing golf last week. He hit this tee shot very far, but it hooked into the rough and he went looking for it He searched all over, but couldn't find it. He kept searching and he found himself next to a cow, actually the butt end of the cow. He can't explain why, but he lifted the cow's tail, and there was a golf ball nestled there. But it wasn't his. He had been playing with a Top-Flite and it was a Titleist. But just then he sees this woman

7

coming over the hill carrying a golf club and looking for her ball.
When she came up next to him and the cow, he raised the cow's tail
and asked, "Hey lady, does this look like yours?", and that's when
she hit him in the throat with her golf club."

Q. What happens to a boy when he reaches puberty?
A. He says good-bye to his boyhood and looks forward to his
adultery.

Q. Name a major disease associated with cigarettes.
A. Premature death.

Q. How can you delay milk turning sour?
A. Keep it in the cow.

Q. How are the main part of the body categorizesd? (e.g., the
abdomen)
A. The body consists of three parts-the brainium, the borax and the
abdomen. The brainium contains the brain, the borax contains the
heart and lungs, and the abdomen contains the five bowels-A,E,I,O
and U.

Q. What is the fibula?
A. A small lie.

Q. What does 'varicose' mean?
A. Nearby

Q. What is the most common form of birth control?
A. Most people prevent contraception by wearing a condominium.

Q. Give the meaning of the term 'Caesarian Section'.
A. The caeserian section is a District in Rome.

Q. What is a seizure?
A. A Roman emperor.

Q. What is a terminal illness?
A. When you are sick at the airport.

Q. What does the word 'benign' mean?
A. Benign is what you will be after you be eight.

Q. What is a turbine?
A. Something an Arab wears on his head.

Q. Give an example of a fungus. What is it's characteristic feature?
A. Mushrooms. They always grow in damp places and so they look like umbrellas.

ANAGRAM

This has got to be one of the cleverest E-mails. Someone out there has too much spare time.

DORMITORY...When you rearrange the letters...DIRTY ROOM

EVANGELIST...When you rearrange the letters...EVIL'S AGENT

PRESBYTERIAN...When you rearrange the letters...BEST IN PRAYER

DESPERATION...When you rearrange the letters...A ROPE ENDS IT

THE MORSE CODE...When you rearrange the letters...HERE COME DOTS

SLOT MACHINES...When you rearrange the letters...CASH LOST IN ME

ANIMOSITY...When you rearrange the letters...NO AMITY

MOTHER-IN-LAW...When you rearrange the letters...WOMAN HITLER

A DECIMAL POINT...When you rearrange the letters...I'M A DOT IN PLACE

SNOOZE ALARM...When you rearrange the letters...ALAS! NO MORE Z'S

ELEVEN PLUS TWO...When you rearrange the letters...
TWELVE PLUS ONE

SUBJECT: THE HUMAN MIND

The phaomnneil pweor of the hmuan mnid.

Aoccdmig to rscheearch at Cmabrigde Uinervtisy, it deosn't mttaer in waht oredr the ltteers in a wrod are, the olny iprmoetnt tihng is taht the frist and the lsat ltteer be at the rghit pclae. The rset can be a taotl mses and you can still raed it wouthit a porbelm. Tihs is bcuseae the huamn mnid deos not raed ervey lteter by istlef, but the wrod as a wlohe. Fcuknig amzanig, huh!

It was opening night at the Orpheum and the Amazing Claude was topping the bill. People came from miles around to see the famed hypnotist do his stuff.

As Claude took to the stage, he announced, "Unlike most stage hypnotists who invite two or three people up onto the stage to be put into a trance, I intend to hypnotize each and every member of the audience."

The excitement was almost electric as Claude withdrew a beautiful antique pocket watch from his coat. "I want you each to keep your eye on this antique watch. It's a very special watch. Its been in my family for six generations." He began to swing the watch gently back and forth while quietly chanting. "Watch the watch, watch the watch, watch the watch..." The crowd became mesmerized as the watch swayed back and forth, light gleaming off its polished surface. Hundred of pairs of eyes followed the swaying watch, until suddenly it slipped from the hypnotist's fingers and fell to the floor, breaking into a hundred pieces.

"S—t!", exclaimed the hypnotist.

It took three weeks to clean up the theater.

Subject: THE RING

A white haired man walked into a jeweler's shop late one Friday, with a beautiful young lady on his side. "I'm looking for a special ring for my girlfriend," he said. The jeweler looks through his stock, and takes out an outstanding ring priced at $5,000. "I don't think you understand…I want something very unique," he said. At that, the jeweler went and fetched his special stock from the safe. "Here's one stunning ring at $40,000." The girl's eyes sparkled, and the man said that he would take it. "How are you paying?" "I'll pay by check, but of course the bank would want to make sure that everything is in order, so I'll write a check and you can phone the bank tomorrow, then I'll fetch the ring on Monday." Monday morning, a very pissed off jeweler phones the man. "You lied, there's no money in that account." "I know, but can you imagine what a fantastic weekend I had," answered the man.

A guy boards a plane for Pittsbugh and sits down in his seat. He notices immediately that the guy next to him has a black eye too. He says to him, "Hey, this is a coincidence, we both have black eyes. Mind if I ask you how you got yours?" He answers, "Well, it was a tongue twister kind of accident. I was at the ticket counter and the girl selling the tickets had these beautiful, big breasts. So, instead of saying, "I'd like a ticket to Pittsburgh', I said, 'I'd like a picket to Tittsburgh. Then she socked me one." I answered, "That's what is called a Freudian Slip. A similar thing happened to me. I was at the breakfast table with my wife. I wanted to say',Please pass the Wheaties', but I accidentally said,'You stupid bitch, you ruined my life.'"

A man walked into the produce section of his local supermarket, and asked to buy half a head of lettuce. The boy working in that department told him that they only sold whole heads of lettuce. The man was insistent that the boy ask his manager about the matter. Walking into the back room, the boy said to the manager, "Some idiot wants to buy half a head of lettuce." As he finished his sentence, he turned to find the man standing right behind him, so he added, "and this gentleman kindly offered to buy the other half."

The manager approved the deal, and the man went on his way. Later the manager said to the boy, "I was impressed with the way you got yourself out of that situation earlier. We like people who think on their feet here. Where are you from, son?" "Texas, sir," the boy replied. "Well, why did you leave Texas?" the manager asked. The boy said, "Sir, there's nothing but whores and football players in Texas." "Really?" said the manager. "My wife is from Texas." "No s—t??" replied the boy. "Who'd she play for?"

HOW TO SPEAK ABOUT WOMEN AND BE POLITICALLY CORRECT:

1. She is not a BABE or a CHICK – She is a BREASTED AMERICAN.

2. She is not a SCREAMER or MOANER – She is VOCALLY APPRECIATIVE.

3. She is not EASY – She is HORIZONTALLY ACCESSIBLE.

4. She is not DUMB – She is a DETOUR OFF THE INFORMATION SUPERHIGHWAY.

5. She has not BEEN AROUND – She is a PREVIOUSLY ENJOYED COMPANION.

6. She is not an AIRHEAD – She is REALITY IMPAIRED.

7. She does not get DRUNK or TIPSY – She gets CHEMICALLY INCONVENIENCED.

8. She is not HORNY – She is SEXUALLY FOCUSED.

9. She does not have BREAST IMPLANTS – She is MEDICALLY ENHANCED.

10. She does not NAG YOU – She becomes VERBALLY REPETITIVE.

11. She is not a SLUT – She is SEXUALLY EXTROVERTED.

12. She does not have MAJOR LEAGUE HOOTERS She is PECTORALLY SUPERIOR.

13. She is not a TWO BIT WHORE – She is a LOW COST PROVIDER.

HOW TO SPEAK ABOUT MEN AND BE POLITICALLY
CORRECT:

1. He does not have a BEER GUT – He has developed a LIQUID
GRAIN STORAGE FACILITY.

2. He is not a BAD DANCER – He is OVERLY CAUCASIAN.

3. He does not GET LOST ALL THE TIME – He
INVESTIGATES ALTERNATIVE DESTINATIONS.

4. He is not BALDING – He is in FOLLICULAR REGRESSION.

5. He is not a CRADLE ROBBER – He prefers
GENERATIONALLY DIFFERENTIAL RELATIONSHIPS.

6. He does not get FALLING-DOWN DRUNK – He becomes
ACCIDENTALLY HORIZONTAL.

7. He does not act like a TOTAL ASS – He develops a case of
RECTAL-CRANIAL INVERSION.

8. He is not a MALE CHAUVINIST PIG – He has SWINE
EMPATHY.

9. He is not afraid of COMMITMENT – He is
MONOGAMOUSLY CHALLENGED

Plan to be spontaneous.

Change is inevitable-except from vending machines.

Honk if you like peace and quiet.

A day without sunshine is like night.

When everything is coming your way, you're in the wrong lane.

If you lend someone $20 and never see that person again, it was probably worth it.

Accept that some days you're the pigeon, and some days you're the statue.

If Barbie is so popular, why do you have to buy her friends?

A SEARCH FOR A SLOGAN

Viagra: It's "Whaazzzz up!"

Viagra: The quicker pecker upper.

Viagra: Like a rock!

Viagra: When it absolutely, positively has to be there tonight,

Viagra: Be all that you can be.

Viagra: Reach out and touch someone.

Viagra: Strong enough for a man, but made for a woman.

Viagra: Tastes great-More filling.

Viagra: We bring good things to life.

Viagra: This is your penis….This is your penis on drugs. Any questions?

Three buddies decided to take their wives on a week's vacation to Las Vegas. The week flew by and they had a great time. After they returned home the men went back to work, and they were sitting around at break and discussing their vacation. The first guy said, "I don't think I'll ever do that again! Ever since we got back, my old lady flings her arms and hollers "seven come eleven" all night, and I haven't had a wink of sleep." The second guy said, "I know what you mean. My old lady played blackjack the whole time we were there and she slaps the bed and hollers "hit me light and hit me hard" and I haven't had a wink of sleep either." The third guy said, "You guys think you have it bad? My old lady played the slots the whole time we were there and I wake up each morning with a sore dick and an ass full of quarters."

A high school English teacher reminds her class of tomorrow's final exam. "Class, I won't tolerate any excuses for you not being there tomorrow. I might consider a nuclear attack or a serious personal injury or illness, or a death in your immediate family – but that's it, no other excuses whatsoever!" A smart-ass guy in the back of the room raises his hand and asks, "What would you say if tomorrow I said I was suffering from complete and utter sexual exhaustion?" The entire class does its best to stifle their laughter and snickering. When silence is restored, the teacher smiles sympathetically at the student, shakes her head, and sweetly says, "Well, I guess you'd have to write the exam with your other hand."

A study conducted by one Department of Psychiatry has revealed that the kind of male face a woman finds attractive can differ depending on where she is in her menstrual cycle. For instance, if she is ovulating she is attracted to men with rugged and masculine features. However, if she is menstruating, or menopausal, she is more prone to be attracted to a man with scissors lodged in his temple and a bat jammed up his ass while he is on fire. Further studies are expected.

An attractive, well dressed woman walks into a shop that sells very expensive Persian rugs. She looks around and spots the perfect rug and walks over to inspect it. As she bends to feel the texture of the rug she farts loudly. Very embarrassed, she looks around nervously to see if anyone has noticed. As she turns back, there standing next to her is a salesman. "Good day Ma'am, how may we help you today?" Very uncomfortably she asks, "Sir, how much does this rug cost?" He answers, "Lady, if you farted just touching it, you're gonna s—t when you hear the price

A man came home from work, sat down in his favorite chair, turned on the TV, and said to his wife, "Quick, bring me a beer before it starts." She looked a little puzzled, but brought him a beer. When he finished it, he said, "Quick, bring me another beer. It's gonna start." This time she looked a little angry, but brought him a beer. When it was gone he said, "Quick, another beer before it starts." "That's it!" She blows her top! "You bastard! You waltz in here, flop your fat ass down, don't even say hello to me and then expect me to run around like your slave. Don't you realize that I cook and clean and wash and iron all day long?" The HUSBAND SIGHED, "ITS STARTED!"

Six retired Floridians were playing poker in the condo clubhouse when Meyerwitz loses $500 on a single hand, clutches his chest and drops dead at the table. Showing respect for their fallen comrade, the other five continue playing standing up. Finkelstein looks around and asks, "So, who's gonna' tell his wife?" They draw straws. Goldberg picks the short one. They tell him to be discreet, be gentle, don't make a bad situation any worse. "Discreet? I'm the most discreet man you will ever meet. Discretion is my middle name, leave it to me."

Goldberg goes over to the Meyerwitz apartment, knocks on the door. The wife answers and asks what he wants. Goldberg declares, "Your husband just lost $500, and is afraid to come home." The wife says, "Tell him to drop dead!" "I'll go tell him," says Goldberg

A man buys several sheep, hoping to breed them for wool. After several weeks, he notices that none of the sheep are getting pregnant, and calls a vet for help. The vet tells him that he should try artificial insemination. The guy doesn't have the slightest idea what this means. Not wanting to display his ignorance, he asks the vet how he will know when the sheep are pregnant. The vet tells him that they will stop standing around and will, instead, lay down and wallow in the grass when they are pregnant. The man hangs up and gives it some thought. He comes to the conclusion that artificial insemination means he himself has to impregnate the sheep. Or course he can't do it on the farm; his wife won't understand. So, he loads the sheep into his truck, drives them out into the woods, has sex with them all, brings them back and goes to bed. Next morning he wakes and looks out at the sheep and notices nary a one is lying down; they are all still standing around. He concludes the first try didn't take and loads them in the truck again. He drives them out to the woods, gets to know them in the Biblical sense – twice for good measure; brings them back and goes to bed. The following morning, he wakes to find the sheep still standing around. One more try, he tells himself, and proceeds to load them up and drive them out to the woods. He spends all day shagging the sheep and, upon returning home, falls listlessly into bed. The next morning, he cannot even raise himself from the bed to look at the sheep. He asks his wife to look out and tell him if the sheep are lying in the grass. "No," she replies, "they're all in the truck and one of them is honking the horn."

Every Sunday, a little old lady placed $1,000 in the collection plate. This went on for weeks until the pastor, overcome by curiosity, approached her. "Ma'am, I couldn't help but notice that you put $1,000 a week in the collection plate," he stated. "Why yes," she replied, "every week my son sends me money, and what I don't need I give to the church." The pastor replied… "That's wonderful, how much does he send you?" The old lady said… "Oh, $20,000 a week." The pastor was amazed… "Your son is very successful, what does he do for a living? "He is a veterinarian," she answered. "That is a very honorable profession," the pastor says. "Where does he practice?" The old lady says proudly... "Well, he has two cat houses in Las Vegas and one in Reno."

A physician claims that the following are actual comments made by his patients (predominately male) while he was performing their colonoscopies:

1. "Take it easy Doc, you're boldly going where no man has gone before."

2. "Find Amelia Earhart yet?"

3. "Can you hear me NOW?"

4. "Oh boy! That was sphincterrfic!"

5. "Are we there yet? Are we there yet? Are we there yet?"

6. "You know in Arkansas we're now legally married."

7. "Any sign of the trapped miners, Chief?"

8. "You put your left hand in, you take your left hand out..."

9. "Hey! Now I know how a Muppet feels!"

10. "If your hand doesn't fit you must quit!"

11. "Hey Doc, let me know if you find my dignity."

12. "You used to be an executive at Enron didn't you?" And the best one of them all...

13. "Could you write a note for my wife saying that my head is in fact not up there."

A young boy asks his father, "Dad, is it OK for us guys to notice all the different kind of boobs?"

Surprised, the father answers, "Well, sure son, we wouldn't be normal if we didn't....There are all kinds of breasts...depending on a woman's age – In her twenties, a woman's breasts are like melons, round and firm. In her thirties to forties, they are like pears, still nice but hanging a bit. After fifty, they are like onions."

"Onions, Dad?"

"Yeah, you see them and they make you cry..."

Not to be outdone, his sister asks her mother, "Mom, how many kind of penises are there?"

The mother, delighted to have equal time, answers, "Well, daughter, a man goes through three phases. In a man's twenties, a man's penis is like an oak, mighty and hard. In his thirties, and forties, it is like a birch, flexible but reliable. After his fifties, it is like a Christmas tree."

"A Christmas tree?"

"Yep, dried up and the balls are only there for decoration..."

A man suffered a serious heart attack and had open heart bypass surgery. He awakened from the surgery to find himself in the care of nuns at a Catholic Hospital. As he was recovering, a nun asked him questions regarding how he was going to pay for his treatment. She asked if he had health insurance. He replied, in a raspy voice, "No health insurance." The nun asked if he had money in the bank. He replied, "No money in the bank." The nun asked, "Do you have a relative who could help you?' He said, "I only have a spinster sister, who is a nun." The nun became agitated and announced loudly, "Nuns are not spinsters! Nuns are married to God!" The patient replied, "In that case, send the bill to my brother-in-law."

Recently, Congress has been debating the ethics of cloning. For many in Congress this is their first experience with the subject. Not with cloning, but ethics....

Answering Machine At A Mental Hospital

Hello, and welcome to the mental health hotline.

If you are obsessive-compulsive, press 1 repeatedly.

If you are codependent, please ask someone to press 2 for you.

If you have multiple personalities, press 3, 4, 5.

If you are paranoid, we know who you are and what you want. Stay on the line so we can trace your call.

If you are delusional, press 7 and your call will be transferred to the mother ship.

If you are schizophrenic, listen carefully and a small voice will tell you which number to press.

If you are a manic-depressive, it doesn't matter which number you press, no one will answer.

If you are dyslexic, press 969696969696969696.

If you have a nervous disorder, please fidget with the pound key until a representative comes on the line.

If you have amnesia, press 8 and state your name, address, telephone number, date of birth, social security number, and your mother's maiden name.

If you have bi-polar disorder, please leave a message after the beep, or before the beep, or after the beep. Please wait for the beep.

If you have short-term memory loss, press 9. If you have short-term memory loss, press 9. If you have short-term memory loss, press 9.

If you have low self-esteem, please hang up. All operators are too busy to talk to you.

If you are blonde don't press any buttons, you'll just screw it up.

Did you hear about the couple who finally became sexually compatible? They achieved simultaneous headaches.

Then there is the story of the woman who goes to her gynecologist and is asked some questions about sexual compatability, "Do you and your husband have mutual orgasms?" She doesn't know, so she calls her husband, then tells the doctor, "No, we have State Farm."

ARTERY ---------------------- The study of painting
BACTERIA -------------------- The back door of the cafeteria
CAT SCAN ------------------- Searching for a kitty
CAUTERIZE ---------------- Made eye contact with her
COLIC ------------------------ A sheep dog
DILATE ---------------------- To live long
ENEMA ---------------------- Not a friend
FESTER ---------------------- Quicker
G.I. SERIES ------------------ A soldier's ball game
IMPOTENT ------------------ Distinguished, well known
LABOR PAIN ---------------- Getting hurt at work
MEDICAL STAFF --------- A doctor's cane
MORBID ---------------------- A higher offer
NITRATES ------------------- Cheaper than day rates
NODE ------------------------- Was aware of
PAP SMEAR ---------------- A fatherhood test
PELVIS ----------------------- A cousin to Elvis
POST OPERATIVE ------- A letter carrier
RECOVERY ROOM ------ A place to do re-upholstery
RECTUM --------------------- Dang near killed 'em
TABLET ---------------------- A small table
TUMOR ---------------------- More than one
URINE ----------------------- Opposite of you're out

The witness was a proper well-dressed elderly lady, the grandmother type, well-spoken and poised. The prosecuting attorney approached the woman and asked, "Mrs. Jones, do you know me?" She responded, "Why, yes, I do know you Mr. Williams. I've known you since you were a young boy and frankly, you've been a big disappointment to me. You lie, cheat on your wife, manipulate people and talk badly about them behind their backs. You think you're a rising big shot when you haven't the sense to realize you never will amount to anything more than a two-bit paper pushing shyster. Yes, I know you quite well." The lawyer was stunned and slowly backed away, fearing the looks on the judge's and juror's faces, not to mention the court reporter who documented every word. Not knowing what else to do, he pointed across the room and asked, "Mrs. Jones, do you know the defense attorney?" She again replied, "Why, yes, I do. I've known Mr. Bradley since he was a youngster, too. He's lazy, bigoted, has a bad drinking problem. The man can't build or keep a normal relationship with anyone and his law practice is one of the worst in the entire state. Not to mention he cheated on his wife with three different women. Yes, I know him." The defense attorney almost fainted and was seen slipping downward in his chair, looking at the floor. Laughter mixed with gasps thundered throughout the court room and the audience was on the verge of chaos.

At this point, the judge brought the courtroom to silence, called both counselors to the bench, and in a very quiet voice said, "If either of you crooked bastards asks her if she knows me, you'll be jailed for contempt."

Energizer Bunny arrested – charged with battery.

A man's home is his castle, in a manor of speaking.

A pessimist's blood type is always b-negative

My wife really likes to make pottery, but to me it's just kiln time.

Dijon vu – the same mustard as before.

Practice safe eating – always use condiments.

I fired my masseuse today. She just rubbed me the wrong way.

A Freudian slip is when you say one thing but mean your mother.

Shotgun wedding A case of wife or death.

I used to work in a blanket factory, but it folded.

I used to be a lumberjack, but I just couldn't hack it, so they gave me the axe.

A man needs a mistress just to break the monogamy.

Marriage is the mourning after the knot before.

A hangover is the wrath of grapes.

Corduroy pillows are making headlines.

Is a book on voyeurism a peeping tome?

Dancing cheek-to-cheek is really a form of floor play.

Sea captains don't like crew cuts.

Does the name Pavlov ring a bell?

A successful diet is the triumph of mind over platter.

Time flies like an arrow. Fruit flies like a banana.

A gossip is someone with a great sense of rumor.

Without geometry, life is pointless.

When you dream in color, it's a pigment of your imagination.

Condoms should be used on every conceivable occasion.

Reading whilst sunbathing makes you well-red.

When two egotists meet, it's an I for an I.

If electricity comes from electrons... does that mean that morality comes from morons?

A backward poet writes inverse.

What's the definition of a will? (It's a dead giveaway.)

In democracy your vote counts. In feudalism your count votes.

She had a boyfriend with a wooden leg, but she broke it off.

A chicken crossing the road is poultry in motion.

If you don't pay your exorcist, you get repossessed.

With her marriage, she got a new name and a dress.

Show me a piano falling down a mine shaft, and I'll show you A flat miner.

When a clock is hungry, it goes back four seconds.

The man who fell into an upholstery machine is fully recovered.

An elderly Italian Jew wanted to unburden his guilty conscience by talking to his Rabbi. "Rabbi, during World War II, when the Germans entered Italy, I pretended to be a Catholic and changed my name from Levy to Spumoni, and I am alive today because of it."

"Self preservation is allowable, and the fact that you never forgot that you were a Jew is admirable," said the Rabbi.

"Rabbi, during the war, a beautiful Jewish woman knocked on my door and asked me to hide her from the Germans. I hid her in my attic, and they never found her."

"That was a wonderful thing you did, and you have no need to feel guilty."

"It's worse, Rabbi. I was weak and told her she must repay me with sexual favors, which she did, repeatedly."

"You were both in great danger and would have suffered terribly if the Germans had found her. There is a favorable balance between good and evil, and you will be judged kindly. Give up your feelings of guilt."

"Thank you, Rabbi. That's a great load off my mind. But I have one more question."

"And what is that?"

"Should I tell her the war is over?"

A few minutes before the church services started, the townspeople were sitting in their pews and talking. Suddenly, Satan appeared at the front of the church. Everyone started screaming and running for the door, trampling each other in a frantic effort to get away from evil incarnate. Soon everyone had exited the church except for one elderly gentleman who sat calmly in his pew without moving, seeming oblivious to the fact that God's ultimate enemy was in his presence.

So Satan walked up to the old man and said; "Don't you know who I am?"

The man replied, "Yep, sure do."

"Aren't you afraid of me?" Satan asked.

"Nope, sure ain't." said the man.

"Don't you realize I can kill you with a glance?" asked Satan.

"Don't doubt it for a minute," returned the old man in an even tone.

"Do you know that I could cause you profound, horrifying AGONY for all eternity?" persisted Satan.

"Yep," was the calm reply.

"And you're still not afraid?" asked Satan.

"Nope," said the old man.

More than a little perturbed, Satan asked, "Well, why aren't you afraid of me?"

The man calmly replied, "Been married to your sister for 48 years."

A Mafia Godfather finds out that his bookkeeper has beat him out of ten million bucks. This bookkeeper is deaf. It was considered an occupational benefit, and why he got the job in the first place, since it was assumed that a deaf bookkeeper would not be able to hear anything he'd ever have to testify about in court.

When the Godfather goes to shakedown the bookkeeper about his missing $10 million bucks, he brings along his attorney, who knows sign language.

The Godfather asks the bookkeeper: "Where is the 10 million bucks you embezzled from me?" The attorney, using sign language, asks the bookkeeper where the 10 million dollars is hidden. The bookkeeper signs back: "I don't know what you are talking about." The attorney tells the Godfather: "He says he doesn't know what you're talking about."

That's when the Godfather pulls out a 9mm pistol, puts it to the bookkeeper's temple, cocks it, and says: "Ask him again!" The attorney signs to the underling: "He'll kill you for sure if you don't tell him!"

The bookkeeper signs back: "OK! You win! The money is in a brown briefcase, buried behind the shed in my cousin Enzio's backyard in Queens!"

The Godfather asks the attorney: "Well, what'd he say?" The attorney replies:

"He says you don't have the balls to pull the trigger"

A Texas cowboy is drinking in a New York bar when he gets a call on his cell phone. He hangs up, grinning from ear to ear, and orders a round of drinks for everybody in the bar because, he announces, his wife has just produced a typical Texas baby boy weighing 25 pounds.

Nobody can believe that any new baby can weigh in at 25 pounds, but the cowboy just shrugs, "That's about average down home, folks...like I said, my boy's a typical Texas baby boy."

Congratulations showered him from all around and many exclamation of "WOW!" were heard. One woman actually fainted due to sympathy pains.

Two weeks later he returns to the bar. The bartender says, "Say, you're the father of that typical Texas baby that weighed 25 pounds at birth, aren't you? Everybody's been making' bets about how big he'd be in two weeks. We were gonna call you! So how much does he weigh now?"

The proud father answers, "Seventeen pounds."

The bartender is puzzled, and concerned. "What happened? He already weighed 25 pounds the day he was born."

The cowboy takes a slow swig from his long-neck beer, wipes his lips on his shirt sleeve, leans into the bartender and proudly says... "Had him circumcised."

A man phoned his doctor late at night saying his wife appeared to have appendicitis.

"That's impossible," the physician replied, peeved at being woken up. "She had an appendectomy last year. Don't be stupid. Only a moron would wake me up for something this idiotic. Have you ever seen anybody with a second appendix?"

"No, you jerk!!!", the husband replied. "Haven't you ever seen anybody with a second wife?"

Working people frequently ask retired people what they do to make their days interesting. I went to the store the other day. I was only in there for about 5 minutes. When I came out there was a city cop writing out a parking ticket. I went up to him and said, "Come on, buddy, how about giving a senior a break?" He ignored me and continued writing the ticket. I called him a Nazi. He glared at me and started writing another ticket for having worn tires. So I called him a piece of horse s—t. He finished the second ticket and put it on the windshield with the first. Then he started writing a third ticket. This went on for about 20 minutes... the more I abused him, the more tickets he wrote. I didn't give a crap. My car was parked around the corner. I try to have a little fun each day now that I'm retired. It's important at my age.

I don't know how they wrote this with a straight face. This was a real memo sent out by a computer company to its employees in all seriousness. It went to all field engineers regarding a computer peripheral problem. The author of this memo was quite genuine. The engineers rolled on the floor!

To whom this may concern

Re: Replacement of Mouse Balls.

If a mouse fails to operate or should it perform erratically, it may need a ball replacement.

Mouse balls are now available as FRU (Field Replacement Units).

Because of the delicate nature of this procedure, replacement of mouse balls should only be attempted by properly trained personnel.

Before proceeding, determine the type of mouse balls by examining the underside of the mouse. Domestic balls will be larger and harder than foreign balls.

Ball removal procedures differ depending upon the manufacturer of the mouse

Foreign balls can be replaced using the pop off method.

Domestic balls are replaced by using the twist off method.

Mouse balls are not usually static sensitive. However, excessive handling can result in sudden discharge.

Upon completion of ball replacement, the mouse may be used immediately.

It is recommended that each person have a pair of spare balls for maintaining optimum customer satisfaction.

Any customer missing his balls should contact the local personnel in charge of removing and replacing these necessary items.

Please keep in mind that a customer without properly working balls is an unhappy customer.

Two deaf people get married. During the first week of marriage, they find that they are unable to communicate in the bedroom with the lights out, since they can't see each other or read lips. After several nights of fumbling around and many misunderstandings, the wife figures out a solution. "Honey, why don't we agree on some simple signals? For instance, at night, if you want to have sex with me, reach over and squeeze my left breast one time. If you don't want to have sex, reach over and squeeze my right breast two times." The husband thinks this is a great idea. He suggests to his wife if she wants to have sex with him, reach over and pull on my penis one time. If you don't want to have sex, pull on my penis two hundred and fifty times."

King Arthur was in Merlin's laboratory where the good wizard was showing him his latest invention. It was a chastity belt, except it had a rather large hole in the most obvious place. "This is no good, Merlin!" the king exclaimed, "Look at this opening. How is this supposed to protect m'lady, the Queen?" "Ah, sire, just observe," said Merlin. He then selected his most worn out wand, one that he was going to discard anyway. He inserted it in the gaping aperture of the chastity belt, whereupon a small guillotine blade came down and cut it neatly in two. "Merlin, you are a genius!" said the grateful monarch. "Now I can leave, knowing that my Queen is fully protected." After putting Guinevere in the device, King Arthur then set out upon his Quest. Several years passed until he returned to Camelot. Immediately he assembled all of his knights in the courtyard and had them drop their trousers for an informal 'short arm' inspection.

Sure enough, each and every one of them was either amputated or damaged in some way. All of them, except Sir Galahad. "Sir Galahad," exclaimed King Arthur. "My one and only true knight! Only you among all the nobles have been true to me. What is it in my power to grant you? Name it and it is yours!" But, alas, Sir Galahad was speechless

Two guys were discussing popular family trends on sex, marriage, and values, Stu said, "I didn't sleep with my wife before we got married, did you?" Leroy replied, "I'm not sure, What was her maiden name?"

A little boy went up to his father and asked: "Dad, where did all of my intelligence come from?" The father replied. "Well son, you must have got it from your mother, cause I still have mine."

"Mr. Clark, I have reviewed this case very carefully," the divorce court Judge said, "And I've decided to give your wife $775 a week," "That's very fair, your honor," the husband said. "And every now and then I'll try to send her a few bucks myself."

A doctor examined a woman, took the husband aside, and said, "I don't like the looks of your wife at all". "Me neither doc," said the husband. "But she's a great cook and really good with the kids.

An old man goes to the Wizard to ask him if he can remove a curse he has been living with for the last 40 years. The Wizard says, "Maybe, but you will have to tell me the exact words that were used to put the curse on you. The old man says without hesitation, "I now pronounce you man and wife."

A blonde calls Delta Airlines and asks, "Can you tell me how long it'll take to fly from San Francisco to New York City?" The agent replies, "Just a minute..." "Thank you." The blonde says, and hangs up.

The Englishman's wife steps up to the tee and, as she bends over to place her ball, a gust of wind blows her skirt up and reveals her lack of underwear. "Good God, woman! Why aren't you wearing any knickers?" her husband demanded. "Well, you don't give me enough housekeeping money to afford any."

The Englishman immediately reaches into his pocket and says, "For the sake of decency, here's $50. Go and buy yourself some underwear." Next, the Irishman's wife bends over to set her ball on the tee. Her skirt also blows up to show that she is wearing no undies. "Blessed Virgin Mary, woman! You've no knickers. Why not?" She replies, "I can't afford any on the money you give me." He reaches into his pocket and says, "For the sake of decency, here's $20. Go and buy yourself some underwear!" Lastly, the Scotsman's wife bends over. The wind also takes her skirt over her head to reveal that she, too, is naked under it "Sweet mudder of Jesus, Aggie! Where the frig are yer drawers?" She too explains, "You dinna give me enough money to be able to affarrd any." The Scotsman reaches into his pocket and says, "Well, fer the love 'o Jasus, 'n the sake of decency, here's a comb. Tidy yerself up a bit."

Snappy Answer #1

A flight attendant was stationed at the departure gate to check-in. As a man approached, she extended her hand for the ticket, and he opened his trench coat and flashed her. Without missing a beat she said, "Sir, I need to see your ticket, not your stub."

Snappy Answer #2

A lady was picking through the frozen turkeys at the grocery store, but couldn't find one big enough for her family. She asked a stock boy, "Do these turkeys get any bigger?" The stock boy replied, "No ma'am, they're dead."

Snappy Answer #3

The cop got out of his car and the kid who was stopped for speeding rolled down his window. "I've been waiting for you all day," the cop said. The kid replied, "Yeah, well I got here as fast as I could." When the cop finally stopped laughing, he sent the kid on his way without a ticket.

Snappy Answer #4

A truck driver was driving along on the freeway. A sign comes up that reads low bridge ahead. Before he knows it the bridge is right ahead of him and he gets stuck under the bridge. Cars are backed up for miles. Finally, a police car comes up. The cop gets out of his car and walks around to the truck driver, puts his hands on his hips and says, "Got stuck, huh?" The truck driver says, "No, I was delivering this bridge and ran out of gas."

Snappy Answer #5

A crowded airline flight was canceled. A single agent was rebooking a long line of inconvenienced travelers. Suddenly an angry passenger pushed his way to the desk. He slapped his ticket down on the counter and said, "I HAVE to be on this flight and it has to be FIRST CLASS." The agent replied, "I'm sorry sir. I'll be happy to try to help you, but I've got to help these folks first, and I'm sure we'll be able to work something out." The passenger was unimpressed. He asked loudly, so that the passengers behind him could hear, "DO YOU HAVE ANY IDEA WHO I AM?" Without hesitating, the agent smiled and grabbed her public address microphone. "May I have your attention please," she began, her voice heard clearly throughout the terminal. "We have a passenger here at Gate 14 WHO DOES NOT KNOW WHO HE IS. If anyone can help him find his identity, please come to Gate 14!" With the folks behind him laughing hysterically, the man glared at the United agent, gritted his teeth and swore, "**Expletive** you!" Without flinching, she smiled and said, "I'm sorry, sir, but you'll have to get in line for that, too."

A college professor gave a lecture on the supernatural. To get a feel for his audience, he asks "How many people here believe in ghosts?" About 90 students raise their hands. "Well, that's a good start. Out of those of you who believe in ghosts, do any of you think you've seen a ghost?" About 40 students raised their hands. "That's really good. I'm really glad you take this seriously. Has anyone here ever talked to a ghost?" About 15 students raise their hands. "Has anyone here ever touched a ghost?" Three students raise their hands. "That's fantastic. Now let me ask you one question further...Have any of you ever made love to a ghost?" Way in the back, Bubba raises his hand. The professor takes off his glasses, and says, "Son, in all the years I've been giving this lecture; no one has ever claimed to have made love to a ghost. You've got to come up here and tell us about your experience." The big redneck student replied with a nod and a grin, and began to make his way up to the podium. When he is at the front of the room, the professor asks, "So, Bubba, tell us what it's like to have sex with a ghost?" Bubba replied, "Shiiiiit! From way back thar I thought you said, 'Goat'!"

A man walks into confessional and says, "Forgive me Father for I have sinned…"

The priest replies, "What is it that brings you here?" "Well father, I used the F-word over the weekend." "Oh, is that all? Say five Hail Marys and may the Lord be with you."

The man replies, "But I really need to talk about it." "Let's have it then," the priest says as he leans back on the hard wooden bench.

"You see Father, I was playing golf this weekend, and on the first tee, I was lining up my drive and proceeded to hit a horrendous slice into the trees."

"And that's when you cursed aloud?" the Father queried. "No, not yet. As luck would have it, I found my ball and had a clear shot to the green from a nice lie; when all of a sudden, a squirrel scampered out of some bushes, picked up my ball by its teeth and darted up a tree."

"That must have been when you cursed?" "No, because just as the squirrel had climbed to the top of the tree, a bird swooped out of the skies and grabbed the squirrel with its talons. The bird flew out of the trees and back out over the green. Then, the squirrel dropped my ball from its mouth, landing 5 inches from the cup!"

"And that's when you cursed aloud," the priest said assuredly. "No, no.."

The Father interjected, "Don't tell me you missed the f----g putt."

ACTUAL BUMPER STICKERS:

I love cats...they taste just like chicken

Out of my mind. Back in five minutes.

Cover me. I'm changing lanes.

As long as there are tests, there will be prayer in public schools

Laugh alone and the world thinks you're an idiot.

Sometimes I wake up grumpy; Other times I let her sleep

I want to die in my sleep like my grandfather... ... Not screaming and yelling like the passengers in his car ...

Montana – At least our cows are sane!

The gene pool could use a little chlorine.

I didn't fight my way to the top of the food chain to be a vegetarian.

Your kid may be an honor student but you're still an IDIOT!

It's as BAD as you think, and they ARE out to get you.

When you do a good deed, get a receipt, in case heaven is like the IRS

Smile, it's the second best thing you can do with your lips.

Friends don't let Friends drive Naked.

Wink, I'll do the rest!

I took an IQ test and the results were negative.

Where there's a will, I want to be in it!

Okay, who stopped the payment on my reality check?

If we aren't supposed to eat animals, why are they made of meat?

Time is the best teacher; Unfortunately it kills all its students!

It's lonely at the top, but you eat better.

Reality? That's where the pizza delivery guy comes from!

Forget about World Peace.....Visualize Using Your Turn Signal!

Warning: Dates in Calendar are closer than they appear.

Give me ambiguity or give me something else.

We are born naked, wet and hungry. Then things get worse.

Make it idiot proof and someone will make a better idiot.

He/She who laughs last thinks slowest

Always remember you're unique, just like everyone else.

Lottery: A tax on people who are bad at math.

Friends help you move. Real friends help you move bodies.

Very funny, Scotty. Now beam down my clothes.

Puritanism: The haunting fear that someone, somewhere may be happy.

Consciousness: that annoying time between naps.

i souport publik edekasion

Be nice to your kids. They'll choose your nursing home.

3 kinds of people: those who can count & those who can't.

Why is "abbreviation" such a long word?

Ever stop to think, and forget to start again?

Diplomacy is the art of saying 'Nice doggie!'...till you can find a rock.

2 + 2 = 5 for extremely large values of 2.

I like you, but I wouldn't want to see you working with subatomic particles.

I killed a 6-pack just to watch it die.

My Harley Davidson climbed Mt. Everest

Visualize Whirled Peas

I'm low on estrogen and I have a gun.

BUMPER STICKERS YOU PROBABLY MISSED BECAUSE YOU WERE DRIVING TOO FAST.

Constipated People Don't Give A Crap.

If You Can Read This, I've Lost My Trailer.

Horn Broken...Watch For Finger.

The Earth Is Full – Go Home.

I Have The Body Of A God – Buddha.

So Many Pedestrians – So Little Time.

Cleverly Disguised As A Responsible Adult.

If We Quit Voting, Will They All Go Away?

Eat Right, Exercise, Die Anyway.

Illiterate? Write For Help.

Honk If Anything Falls Off.

He Who Hesitates Not Only Is Lost, But is Miles From The Next Exit.

I Refuse To Have A Battle Of Wits With An Unarmed Person.

You! Out Of The Gene Pool – Now!

I Do Whatever My Rice Krispies Tell Me To.

Fight Crime: Shoot Back!

(Seen Upside Down On A Jeep) If You Can Read This, Please Flip Me Back Over...

Stop Lights Timed For 35 mph Also Are Timed For 70 mph

Guys: No Shirt, No Service

Gals: No Shirt, No Charge

If Walking Is So Good For You, Then Why Does My Mailman Look Like Jabba The Hut?

Ax Me About Ebonics.

Body By Nautilus; Brain By Mattel.

Boldly Going Nowhere.

Caution – Driver Legally Blonde.

Heart Attacks: God's Revenge For Eating His Animal Friends

Honk If You've Never Seen An Uzi Fired From A Car Window.

How Many Roads Must A Man Travel Down Before He Admits He is Lost?

GROW YOUR OWN DOPE --- PLANT A MAN.

All Men Are Animals; Some Just Make Better Pets.

AND THE GREATEST BUMPER STICKER EVER: "POLITICIANS & DIAPERS BOTH NEED TO BE CHANGED, AND FOR THE SAME REASON"

NEW DRUGS FOR WOMEN!

ST. MOM'S WORT: Plant extract that treats mom's depression by rendering preschoolers unconscious for up to six hours.

EMPTY NESTROGEN: Highly effective supplement that eliminates melancholy by enhancing the memory of how awful they were as teenagers and how you couldn't wait till they moved out.

PEPTO-BIMBO: Liquid silicone for single women. Two full cups swallowed before an evening out increases breast size, decreases intelligence, and improves flirting.

DUMMEROL: When taken with Pepto-bimbo, can cause lowering of IQ, causing enjoyment of loud country music and cheap beer.

FLIPITOR: Increases life expectancy of commuters by controlling road rage and the urge to flip off other drivers.

JACKASSPIRIN: Relieves headache caused by a man who can't remember your birthday, anniversary, or phone number.

RAGAMET: When administered to a husband, provides the same irritation as nagging on him all weekend, saving the wife the time and trouble of doing it herself.

DAMMITOL: Take two and the rest of the world can go to hell for 8 hours!

ANTI-TALKSIDENT: A spray carried in a purse or wallet to be used on anyone too eager to share their life stories with total strangers.

BUYAGRA: Stimulant to be taken prior to shopping. Increases potency and duration of spending spree.

MENICILLN: Potent anti-boy-otic for older women. Increases resistance to such lines as, "You make me want to be a better person. Can we get naked now?"

Here are the 10 first place winners in the International Pun Contest

1. A vulture boards an airplane, carrying two dead raccoons. The stewardess looks at him and says, "I'm sorry, sir, only one carrion allowed per passenger."

2. Two fish swim into a concrete wall. The one turns to the other and says "Dam!"

3. Two Eskimos sitting in a kayak were chilly, so they lit a fire in the craft. Unsurprisingly it sank, proving once again that you can't have your kayak and heat it too.

4. Two hydrogen atoms meet. One says "I've lost my election." The other says "Are you sure?" The first replies "Yes, I'm positive."

5. Did you hear about the Buddhist who refused Novocain during a root canal? His goal: transcend dental medication.

6. A group of chess enthusiasts checked into a hotel and were standing in the lobby discussing their recent tournament victories. After about an hour they were thrown out of the lobby by the manager. "Why?" they asked, as they moved off. "Because", he said, "I can't stand chess-nuts boasting in an open foyer."

7. A woman has twins and gives them up for adoption. One of them goes to a family in Egypt and is named "Ahmal." The other goes to a family in Spain; they name him "Juan." Years later, Juan sends a picture of himself to his birth mother. Upon receiving the picture, she tells her husband that she wishes she also had a picture of Ahmal. Her husband responds, "They're twins! If you've seen Juan, you've seen Ahmal."

8. These friars were behind on their belfry payments, so they opened up a small florist shop to raise funds. Since everyone liked to buy flowers from the men of God, a rival florist across town thought the competition was unfair. He asked the good fathers to close down, but they would not.

He went back and begged the friars to close. They ignored him. So, the rival florist hired Hugh MacTaggart, the roughest and most vicious thug in town to "persuade" them to close. Hugh beat up the friars and trashed their store, saying he'd be back if they didn't close up shop. Terrified, they did so, thereby proving that only Hugh, can prevent florist friars.

9. Mahatma Gandhi, as you know, walked barefoot most of the time, which produced an impressive set of calluses on his feet. He also ate very little, which made him rather frail and with his odd diet, he suffered from bad breath. This made him…(Oh, man, this is so bad, it's good)….A super calloused fragile mystic hexed by halitosis.

10. And finally, there was the person who sent ten different puns to his friends, with the hope that at least one of the puns would make them laugh. No pun in ten did!

A grenade thrown into a kitchen in France would result in Linoleum Blownapart.

You feel stuck with your debt if you can't budge it.

Local Area Network in Australia: the LAN down under.

He often broke into song because he couldn't find the key.

A lot of money is tainted – It taint yours and it taint mine.

A boiled egg in the morning is hard to beat.

A plateau is a high form of flattery.

The short fortuneteller who escaped from prison was a medium at large.

Those who get too big for their britches will be exposed in the end.

Once you've seen one shopping center, you've seen a mall.

Those who jump off a Paris bridge are in Seine.

When an actress saw her first strands of gray hair, she thought she'd dye.

Bakers trade bread recipes on a knead-to-know basis.

Santa's helpers are subordinate clauses.

Acupuncture is a jab well done.

Marathon runners with bad footwear suffer the agony of defeet.

These are the only ten times in history the "F" word has been acceptable for use...

10. "What the @#$% was that?"-Mayor Of Hiroshima, 1945

9. "Where did all those @#$%ing Indians come from?"-Custer, 1877

8. "Any @#$%ing idiot could understand that."-Einstein, 1938

7. "It does so @#$%ing look like her!"-Picasso, 1926

6. "How the @#$% did you work that out?"-Pythagoras, 126 BC

5. "You want WHAT painted on the @#$%ing ceiling?"-Michelangelo, 1566

4. "Where the @#$% are we?"-Amelia Earhart, 1937

3. "Scattered @#$%ing showers....my ass!"-Noah, 4314BC

2. "Aw, c'mon. Who the @#$% is going to find out?"-Bill Clinton, 1999

1. "What the @#$% do you mean we're sinking?"-Captain of the Titanic-1912

One day a man came home and was greeted by his wife dressed in a very sexy nightie. "Tie me up," she purred, "and you can do anything you want." So, he tied her up and went golfing.

Paul was shopping the other day and wound up face to face with this drop dead gorgeous woman. He couldn't help but just stare at her, so much so that his mouth dropped open and he was drooling. The woman caught him staring and suspected he wasn't just admiring her outfit. She said, "Are you often troubled by indecent thoughts?" Paul replied, "No, ma'am. Actually, to be honest, I rather enjoy them."

When Morris gets home from work, Sara his wife tells him, "So today I went to the doctor and he says I can't make love." Morris asks, "How'd he find out?"

If you jog in a jogging suit, lounge in lounging pajamas, and smoke in a smoking jacket, WHY would anyone want to wear a windbreaker??

A Woman's Fantasy

A man is in a hotel lobby. He wants to ask the clerk a question.
As he turns to go to the front desk, he accidentally bumps into a
woman beside him and as he does, his elbow grazes her breast.
They are both quite startled. The man turns to her and says,
"Ma'am, if your heart is as soft as your breast, I know you'll
forgive me." She replies, "if your penis is as hard as your elbow,
I'm in room 436."

A Man's Fantasy

A man walks into a building and gets into the lift. He presses
the button for the fifth floor. At the fifth floor the most stunning
woman he has ever seen gets into the lift and leans seductively
against the wall. The man doesn't know where to look and starts
to get very nervous. The woman begins to unbutton her blouse and
throws it on the floor. She then takes off her bra and throws it on
the floor. At this stage the guy is getting very nervous. Then she
says "Make a woman out of me". He unbuttons his shirt, throws it
on the floor and replies – "Iron that!"

Now that I'm 'older' (but refuse to grow up), here's what I've discovered:

ONE - I started out with nothing, and I still have most of it left.

TWO – My wild oats have turned into prunes and All Bran.

THREE – I finally got my head together; now my body is falling apart.

FOUR – Funny, I don't remember being absent minded…

FIVE – All reports are in; life is now officially unfair.

SIX – If all is not lost, where is it?

SEVEN – It is easier to get older than it is to get wiser.

EIGHT – Some days you're the dog; some days you're the hydrant.

NINE – I wish the buck stopped here; I sure could use a few…

TEN – Kids in the back seat cause accidents.

ELEVEN – Accidents in the back seat cause kids.

TWELVE – It's hard to make a comeback when you haven't been anywhere.

THIRTEEN – The only time the world beats a path to your door is when you're in the bathroom.

FOURTEEN – If God wanted me to touch my toes, he would have put them on my knees.

FIFTEEN – When I'm finally holding all the cards, why does everyone decide to play chess?

SIXTEEN – It's not hard to meet expenses…they're everywhere.

SEVENTEEN – The only difference between a rut and a grave is the depth.

EIGHTEEN – These days, I spend a lot of time thinking about the hereafter…I go somewhere to get something and then wonder what I'm here after.

NINETEEN – I AM UNABLE TO REMEMBER IF I HAVE MAILED THIS TO YOU BEFORE

At Last, a Dr. Seuss for Seniors.

DR SEUSS ON AGING

I cannot see

I cannot pee

I cannot chew

I cannot screw

Oh, my God, what can I do?

My memory shrinks

My hearing stinks

No sense of smell

I look like hell

My mood is bad – can't you tell?

My body's drooping

Have trouble pooping

The Golden Years have come at last

The Golden Years can kiss my ass

THE MEANING OF PHRASES CHANGES AS ONE'S AGE CHANGES

The meaning of certain phrases changes depending on your age. In college an 'all-nighter' meant studying all night for an exam. Later it meant having sex all night. Now it means sleeping through the night without having to get up to go to the bathroom.

A young man once asked God how long a million years was to him. – God replied, "A million years to me is just like a single second to you."

The young man asked God what a million dollars was to him. – God replied, "A million dollars to me is just like a single penny to you."

Then the young man got his courage up and asked, "God, could I have one of your pennies?" – God smiled and replies, "Certainly, just a second."

A drunk was proudly showing off his new apartment to a couple of his friends late one night. When they made it to the bedroom, they saw a big brass gong next to the bed. "What's a big brass gong doing in your bedroom?" one of the guests asked. "It's not a gong. It's a talking clock," the drunk replied. "A talking clock? Seriously?" asked his astonished friend. "Yup," replied the drunk. "How's it work?" the friend asked, squinting at it. "Watch," the drunk replied. He picked up the mallet, gave the gong an ear-shattering whack, and stepped back. The three stood looking at one another for a moment. Suddenly, someone on the other side of the wall screamed, "You a------e, it's ten past three in the morning!"

A woman was in a coma. Nurses were in her room giving her a sponge bath. One of them was washing her private area and noticed that there was a response on the monitor when she touched her. They went to her husband and explained what happened, telling him, "Crazy as this sounds, maybe a little oral sex will do the trick and bring her out of the coma. The husband was skeptical, but they assured him that they'd close the curtains for privacy. The hubby finally agreed and went into his wife's room. After a few minutes the woman's monitor flat lined, no pulse, no heart rate. The nurses ran into the room. "What happened?" they cried. The husband said, "I guess she choked."

A woman meets a Navy chief in a bar. They talk; they connect; they end up leaving together. They go back to his place. As he shows her around his apartment, she is struck by the fact that his bedroom is completely packed with sweet, cuddly teddy bears. There are literally hundreds of teddybears on three shelves running the length of the room along one wall. Small, adorable teddy bears fill the bottom shelf. Cute, cuddly medium-sized ones adorn a shelf a little higher. Huge enormous bears are perched on the top shelf along the wall. The woman is quite surprised that a chief would have a collection of teddy bears, especially one that's so extensive. Although she decides not to question him about it, she actually is quite impressed by this unexpected evidence of his sensitive side!

She turns to him, invitingly.......they kiss softly.......then again. Soon their passion has overwhelmed them, and she leads him quietly to the huge king –size bed along the far wall. After spending an intense night of passion with the chief, and they are lying there together in the afterglow, the woman slowly rolls toward him and asks "How was it for you"? The chief, stifling a slight yawn replies: "Help yourself to any prize from the bottom shelf."

Ken's last request…Ken was on his deathbed and gasped pitifully. "Promise to fulfill my last request, Cindy," he said. "Of course, Ken," his wife said softly. "Six months after I die," he said, "I want you to marry Tim." "But I thought you hated Tim," she said. With his last breath, Ken said, "I do!"

A Captain in the foreign legion was transferred to a desert outpost. On his orientation tour he noticed a very old, seedy looking camel tied out back of the enlisted men's barracks. He asked the Sergeant leading the tour, "What's the camel for?" The Sergeant replied, "Well sir, the fort's a long way from anywhere, and the men have natural sexual urges, so when they do, we have the camel." The Captain said "Well, if it's good for morale, then I guess it's all right with me."

After he had been at the fort for about 6 months, the Captain could not stand it anymore, so he told his Sergeant, "BRING IN THE CAMEL!!!" The Sergeant shrugged his shoulders and led the camel into the Captain's quarters. The Captain got a foot stool and proceeded to have vigorous sex with the camel. As he stepped, satisfied, down from the stool and was buttoning his pants he asked the Sergeant, "Is that how the enlisted men do it?" The Sergeant replied, "Well sir, they usually just use it to ride into town."

Sherry the secretary walked into her boss's office and said, "I'm afraid I've got some bad news for you" "Sherry, honey, why do you always have to give me bad news?" he complained. "Tell me some good news for once." "Alright, here's some good news," said the secretary. "You're not sterile."

Jim: "Joe, I hear you just got married again."

Joe: "Yes, for the fourth time."

Jim: "What happened to your first three wives?"

Joe: "They all died, Jim."

Jim: "How did that happen?"

Joe: "My first wife ate poison mushrooms."

Jim: "How terrible! And your second?"

Joe: "She ate poison mushrooms."

Jim: "And your third ate poison mushrooms too?"

Joe: "Oh, no. She died of a broken neck."

Jim: "I see, an accident."

Joe: "Not exactly. She wouldn't eat her mushrooms."

Attending a wedding for the first time, a little girl whispered to her mother, "Why is the bride dressed in white?" "Because white is the color of happiness, and today is the happiest day of her life." The child thought about this for a moment, then said, "So why is the groom wearing black?"

An elderly woman died last month. Having never married, she requested no male pallbearers. In her handwritten instructions for her memorial service, she wrote, "They wouldn't take me out while I was alive, I don't want them to take me out when I'm dead.

A police recruit was asked during the exam, "What would you do if you had to arrest your own mother?" He said, "Call for backup."

A Sunday school teacher was discussing the Ten Commandments with her five and six year olds. After explaining the commandment to "honor thy father and thy mother," she asked "Is there a commandment that teaches us how to treat our brothers and sisters?" Without missing a beat one little boy answered, "Thou shall not kill."

1. Ratio of an igloo's circumference to its diameter = Eskimo Pi

2. 2000 pounds of Chinese soup = Won ton

3. 1 millionth of a mouthwash = 1 microscope

4. Time between slipping on a peel and smacking the pavement = 1 bananosecond

5. Weight an evangelist carries with God = 1 billigram

6. Time it takes to sail 220 yards at 1 nautical mile per hour = 1 Knotfurlong

7. 365.25 days of drinking low calorie beer = 1 Lite year

8. 16.5 feet in the Twilight Zone = 1 Rod Serling

9. Half a large intestine = 1 semicolon

10. 1,000,000 aches = 1 megahurtz

11. Basic unit of laryngitis = 1 hoarsepower

12. Shortest distance between two jokes – a straight line

13. 453.6 graham crackers = 1 pound cake

14. 1 million microphones = 1 megaphone

15. 1 million bicycles = 1 megacycles

16. 365.25 = 1 unicycle

17. 2000 mockingbirds = two kilomockingbirds

18. 10 cards = 1 decacard

19. 52 cards = 1 deckacard

20. 1 kilogram of falling figs = 1 fig Newton

21. 1000 grams of wet socks = 1 literhosen

22. 1 millionth of a fish = 1 microfiche

23. 1 trillion pins = 1 terrapin

24. 10 rations = 1 decaration

25. 100 rations = 1 C-ration

26. 2 monograms = 1 diagram

27. 8 nickels = 2 paradigms

28. 2.4 statute miles of intravenous surgical tubing at Yale University Hospital = 1 I.V. League

Due to inherit a fortune when his sickly, widower father died, Bob decided he needed a woman to enjoy it with. So he went to a singles bar and he searched until he spotted a woman whose beauty took his breath away.

"Right now, I'm just an ordinary man," he said, walking up to her, "but within a month or two, my father will pass and I'll inherit over 20 million dollars."

The woman went home with Bob, and four days later she became his stepmother. Men will never learn.

A three year old little boy was examining his testicles while taking a bath. "Mama," he asked, "Are these my brains?" Mama answered, "Not yet."

BEDTIME POEMS
For BIG Kids

JACK AND JILL Went up the hill To have a little fun.
Stupid Jill forgot the pill
And now they have a son.

MARY HAD A LITTLE LAMB
Her father shot it dead.
Now it goes to school with her,
Between two hunks of bread.

LITTLE MISS MUFFET sat on a tuffet.
Her clothes all tattered and torn.
It wasn't the spider that crept up beside her,
But Little Boy Blue and his horn.

SIMPLE SIMON met a Pie man going to the fair.
Said Simple Simon to the Pie man,
"What have you got there?"
Said the Pie man unto Simon.
"Pies, you idiot!"

HUMPTY DUMPTY sat on a wall,
Humpty Dumpty had a great fall.
All the kings' horses,
And all the kings' men.
Had scrambled eggs,
For breakfast again.

HEY DIDDLE, DIDDLE the cat took a piddle,

All over the bedside clock.

The little dog laughed to see such fun.

Then died of electric shock.

GEORGIE PORGY Pudding and Pie,

Kissed the girls and made them cry.

And when the boys came out to play,

He kissed them too 'cause he was gay.

There was a little girl who had a little curl

Right in the middle of her forehead.

When she was good, she was very, very good.

But when she was bad......

She got a fur coat, jewels, a waterfront condo, and a sports car.

The difference between now and 30 years ago

1973: Disco
2003: Costco

1973: Long hair
2003: Longing for hair

1973: KEG
2003: EKG

1973: Acid rock
2003: Acid reflux

1973: Moving to California because it's cool
2003: Moving to California because it's warm

1973: Growing pot
2003: Growing pot belly

1973: Passing the driver's test
2003: Passing the vision test

1973: Seeds and stems
2003: Roughage

1973: Killer weed
2003: Weed killer

1973: Hoping for a BMW
2003: Hoping for a BM

1973: The Grateful Dead
2003: Dr. Kevorkian

1973: Going to a new, hip joint
2003: Receiving a new hip joint

1973: Rolling Stones
2003: Kidney Stones

1973: Being called into the principal's office
2003: Calling the principal's office

1973: Screw the system
2003: Upgrade the system

Gerry is enjoying a good game of golf with her girlfriends one day. She is having such a good time and playing so well that she loses track of time.

"Oh, no! I have to rush home and fix dinner for my husband! He's going to be really ticked if it's not ready on time." When she gets home, she realized she doesn't have enough time to go to the supermarket, and all she has in the cupboard is a wilted lettuce leaf, an egg and a can of cat food. In a panic, she opens the can of cat food, stirs in the egg and garnished it with the lettuce leaf just as her husband is pulling up. She greets her husband and then watches in horror as he sits down to his dinner. To her surprise, her husband is really enjoying his dinner.

"Darling, this is the best dinner you have made for me in forty years of marriage. You can make this for me any old day."

Needless to say, every day from then on, the woman made her husband the same dish. She told her golf partners about it and they were all horrified. "You're going to kill him!" they exclaimed. Two months later, her husband died. The women were sitting around when one of them said, "You killed him! We told you that feeding him that cat food every week would do him in! How can you just sit there so calmly knowing you murdered your husband?"

The wife stoically replied, "I didn't kill him. He fell off the window sill while he was licking his ass."

A very genteel Southern lady was driving across the Savannah River Bridge in Augusta, GA one day. As she neared the top of the bridge, she noticed a young man standing near the edge of the bridge getting ready to jump.

She stopped her car, rolled down her window and said, "Please don't jump, think of your Mother and Father." He replied, "My Mom and Dad are both dead, I'm gonna jump." She said, "Well, think of your wife and children." He replied, "I'm not married and I don't have any kids." She said, "Well, then think of Robert E. Lee." He replied, "Who is Robert E. Lee?" She replied, "Well, just go on and jump, you Yankee bastard

A woman awakes during the night to find that her husband is not in bed. She puts on her robe and goes downstairs to look for him. She finds him sitting at the kitchen table with a cup of coffee in front of him.

He appears to be in deep thought, just staring at the wall. She watches as he wipes a tear from his eye and takes a sip of his coffee. "What's the matter, dear?" she whispers as she steps into the room, "Why are you down here at this time of night?" The husband looks up from his coffee. "Do you remember 20 years ago when we were dating, and you were only 15?" he asks solemnly.

"Yes I do," she replies. The husband pauses. The words are not coming easily. "Do you remember when your father caught us in the back seat of my car?" "Yes, I remember," says the wife, lowering herself into a chair beside him. The husband continues. "Do you remember when he shoved the shotgun in my face and said, either you marry my daughter, or I'll send you to jail for 20 years?" "I remember that too," she replies softly. He wipes another tear from his cheek and says, "I would have gotten out today."

A man comes home from a tough day of work looking to unwind. After a relaxing dinner with his wife, they retire to their twin beds. However, the man was not yet ready to slumber, and called over to his wife. "My little boopey-boo, I'm lonely." So the woman gets out of bed and crosses the room to the husband. On the way, she trips on the carpet and falls on her face. The husband, with a concerned look on his face says, "Oh, did my little honey-bunny fall on her little nosey-wosey?" The woman just smiles, gets up and enters hubby's bed. The two have passionate sex and afterwards the woman rolls out. As she is returning to her bed, she once again catches her foot on the carpet and falls flat on her face. The man looks over his shoulder at his wife lying on the floor and says, "Clumsy bitch."

Paddy and his two friends are talking at a bar. His first friend says, "I think my wife is having an affair with the electrician. The other day I came home and found wire cutters under our bed and they weren't mine."

His second friend says "I think my wife is having an affair with the plumber, the other day I found a pipe-wrench under the bed and it wasn't mine."

Paddy says, "I think my wife is having an affair with a horse." Both his friends look at him with utter disbelief. "I'm serious. The other day I came home and found a jockey under our bed."

A couple of women were playing golf one sunny Saturday morning. The first of the twosome teed off and watched in horror as her ball headed directly toward a foursome of men playing the next hole. Indeed, the ball hit one of the men, and he immediately clasped his hands together at his crotch, fell to the ground and proceeded to roll around in evident agony. The woman rushed down to the man and immediately began to apologize. She explained that she was a physical therapist: "Please allow me to help. I'm a physical therapist and I know I could relieve your pain if you'd allow me!", she told him earnestly. "Ummph, oooh, nnooo, I'll be alright...I'll be fine in a few minutes", he replied breathlessly as he remained in the fetal position still clasping his hands together at his crotch. But she persisted, and he finally allowed her to help him. She gently took his hands away and laid them to the side, she loosened his pants, and she put her hands inside. She began to massage him. She then asked him: "How does that feel?" To which he replied: "It feels great, but my thumb still hurts like hell."

Why Athletes Can't Have Real Jobs, and should never try to inspire kids.

Chicago Cubs outfielder on being a role model: "I wan' all dem kids to do what I do, to look up to me. I wan' all the kids to copulate me."

New Orleans Saint RB when asked about the upcoming season: "I want to rush for 1,000 or 1,500 yards, whichever comes first."

A Redskins player said: "I'd run over my own mother to win the Super Bowl," Another player said: "I'd run over his mom, too."

A University of Houston receiver, on his coach: "He treats us like men. He lets us wear earrings."

Football commentator and former player: "Nobody in football should be called a genius. A genius is a guy like Norman Einstein."

Senior basketball player at the University of Pittsburgh: "I'm going to graduate on time, no matter how long it takes." (now that is beautiful)

A Florida State football coach: "You guys line up alphabetically by height." And, "You guys pair up in groups of three, then line up in a circle."

Boxing promoter Dan Duva on Mike Tyson hooking up again with promoter Don King: "Why would anyone expect him to come out smarter? He went to prison for three years, not Princeton."

A Chicago Blackhawks hockey player, explaining why he keeps a color photo of himself above his locker: "That's so when I forget how to spell my name, I can still find my clothes."

A veteran boxing trainer, on the Spartan training regime of one of his heavyweights: "He's a guy who gets up at six o'clock in the morning regardless of what time it is."

A North Carolina State basketball player, explaining to his coach why he appeared nervous at practice: "My sister's expecting a baby, and I don't know if I'm going to be an uncle or an aunt." (I wonder if his IQ ever hit room temperature in January)

A basketball team executive on a former player: "I told him, 'Son, what is it with you? Is it ignorance or apathy?' He said, 'Coach, I don't know and I don't care."

A college basketball coach recounting what he told a player who received four F's and one D: "Son, looks to me like you're spending too much time on one subject."

Several men are in the locker room of a golf club when a mobile phone on a bench starts to ring. Sidney picks it up, engages the hands free speak-function and begins to talk. "Hello," says Sidney. "Honey, it's me," says a woman, "are you at the club?" "Yes," replies Sidney. "Well I'm at the shopping mall," she says, "and I've found a beautiful leather coat. It's $450. Can I buy it?" "OK," says Sidney, "go ahead and buy it if you like it that much." "Thanks," she replies. "I also stopped by the Mercedes dealership and had a close look at the new models. I saw one that I really liked." "How much was it?" asks Sidney. "$47,000," she replied. "For that price," says Sidney, "I want it with all the options." "Great," she says. "Just one more thing. That house we wanted last year is back on the market. They're only asking $750,000 for it now." Sidney says, "Well then, go ahead and buy it, but don't offer more than $720,000." "OK," she says, "I'll see you later. I love you." "Bye, I love you too." says Sidney and then hangs up. The other men in the locker room who heard all of this conversation are looking at Sidney in astonishment. Then Sidney shouts out aloud, "Does anyone know who this cell phone belongs to?"

It's the Spring of 1957 and Bobby goes to pick up his date, Peggy Sue. Bobby's a pretty hip guy with his own car and a ducktail hairdo. When he goes to the front door, Peggy Sue's father answers and invites him in.

"Peggy Sue's not ready yet, so why don't you have a seat?" he says. "That's cool." Says Bobby.

Peggy Sue's father asks Bobby what they are planning to do. Bobby replies politely that they will probably just go to the malt shop or to a drive-in movie.

Peggy Sue's father responds "Why don't you kids go out and screw? I hear all of the kids are doing it."

Naturally this comes as quite a surprise to Bobby and he says "Whaaaat?"

"Yeah," says Peggy Sue's father, "Peggy Sue really likes to screw; she'll screw all night if we let her!"

Bobby's eyes light up and smiles from ear to ear. Immediately, he has revised the plans for the evening. A few minutes later, Peggy Sue comes downstairs in her little poodle skirt with her saddle shoes and announces that she's ready to go.

Almost breathless with anticipation, Bobby escorts his date out the front door while dad is saying "Have a good evening kids," with a wink for Bobby.

About 20 minutes later, a thoroughly disheveled Peggy Sue rushes back into the house, slams the door behind her and screams at her father" "DAMMIT DADDY! THE TWIST!!!IT'S CALLED THE TWIST!!!"

Subject: Top 10 Golf Caddy Comments

10. Golfer: "I think I'm going to drown my self in the lake."
Caddy: "Think you can keep your head down that long?"

9. Golfer: "I'd move heaven and earth to break 100 on this course."
Caddy: "Try heaven, you've already moved most of the earth."

8. Golfer: "Do you think my game is improving?"
Caddy: "Yes sir, you miss the ball much closer now."

7. Golfer: "Do you think I can get there with a 5 iron?"
Caddy: "Eventually."

6. Golfer: "You've got to be the worst caddy in the world."
Caddy: "I don't think so sir. That would be too much of a coincidence."

5. Golfer: "Please stop checking your watch all the time. It's too much of a distraction."
Caddy: "It's not a watch – it's a compass."

4. Golfer: "How do you like my game?"
Caddy: "Very good sir, but personally, I prefer golf."

3. Golfer: "Do you think it's a sin to play on Sunday?"
Caddy: "The way you play, sir, it's a sin on any day."

2. Golfer: "This is the worst course I've ever played on."
Caddy: "This isn't the golf course. We left that an hour ago,"

1. Golfer: "That can't be my ball, it's too old."
Caddy: "It's been a long time since we teed off, sir."

HE SAID.............SHE SAID

1)He said....I don't know why you wear a bra, you've got nothing to put in it.
She said....You wear briefs, don't you?

2)She said....What do you mean by coming home half drunk?
He said....It's not my fault...I ran out of money.

3)He said....Since I first laid eyes on you I've wanted to make love to you in the worst way.
She said...Well, you succeeded.

4)He said.....Two inches more, and I would be king.
She said....Two inches less, and you'd be queen.

5)On wall in ladies room....My husband follows me everywhere.
Written below it....I do not.

6)He said......Shall we try a different position tonight?
She said.....That's a good idea...you stand by the ironing board while I sit on the sofa and fart.

7)Priest....I don't think you will ever find another man like your late husband.
She said....Who's gonna look?

8)He said...What have you been doing with all the grocery money I gave you?
She said....Turn sideways and look in the mirror.

9)He said....Let's go out and have some fun tonight.
She said.....Okay, but if you get home before I do, leave the hallway light on.

10)He said...Why don't you tell me when you have an orgasm?
She said....I would...but you're never there.

The following questions and answers were collated from SAT tests given in 2000 to 16 year old students.

Q. Name the four seasons.
A. Salt, pepper, mustard and vinegar.

Q. Explain one of the processes by which water can be made safe to drink.
A. Filtration makes water safe to drink because it removes large pollutants like grit, sand, dead sheep and canoeists.

Q. How is dew formed?
A. The sun shines down on the leaves and makes them perspire.

Q. What is a planet?
A. A body of earth surrounded by sky.

Q. What causes the tides in the ocean?
A. The tides are a fight between the Earth and the Moon. All water tends to flow towards the moon, because there is no water on the moon, and nature abhors a vacuum. I forget where the sun joins in this fight.

Q. In a democratic society, how important are elections?
A. Very important. Sex can only happen when a male gets an election.

Q. What happens to your body as you age?
A. When you get old, so do your bowels and you get intercontintal.

"Senior" personal ads

Some "Senior" personal ads seen in Florida newspapers: (Who says seniors don't have a sense of humor?)

FOXY LADY: Sexy, fashion-conscious blue-haired beauty, 80's, slim, 5'4" (use to be 5'6"), searching for sharp-looking, sharp-dressing companion. Matching white shoes and belt a plus.

LONG-TERM COMMITMENT: Recent widow who has just buried fourth husband, and am looking for someone to round out a six-unit plot. Dizziness, fainting, shortness of breath not a problem.

SERENITY NOW: I am into solitude, long walks, sunrises, the ocean, yoga and meditation. If you are the silent type, let's get together, take our hearing aids out and enjoy quiet times.

WINNING SMILE: Active grandmother with original teeth seeking a dedicated flosser to share rare steaks, corn on the cob and caramel candy.

BEATLES OR STONES? I still like to rock, still like to cruise in my Camaro on Saturday nights and still like to play the guitar. If you were a groovy chick, or are now a groovy hen, let's get together and listen to my eight-track tapes.

MEMORIES: I can usually remember Monday through Thursday. If you can remember Friday, Saturday and Sunday, let's put our two heads together.

MINT CONDITION: Male, 1932, high mileage, good condition, some hair, many new parts including hip, knee, cornea, valves. Isn't in running condition, but walks well.

1. Now that food has replaced sex in my life, I can't even get into my own pants.

2. Marriage changes passion. Suddenly you're in bed with a relative.

3. I saw a woman wearing a sweat shirt with "Guess" on it. So I said "Implants?" She hit me.

4. I don't do drugs. I get the same effect just standing up fast.

5. Sign in a Chinese Pet Store: "Buy one dog, get one flea..."

6. I live in my own little world. But it's OK. They know me here.

7. I got a sweater for Christmas. I really wanted a screamer or a moaner.

8. If flying is so safe, why do they call the airport the terminal?

9. I don't approve of political jokes. I've seen too many of them get elected.

10. There are two sides to every divorce: Yours and shithead's.

11. I love being married. It's so great to find that one special person you want to annoy for the rest of your life.

12. I am a nobody, and nobody is perfect; therefore, I am perfect.

13. Everyday I beat my own previous record for the number of consecutive days I've stayed alive.

14. How come we choose from just two people to run for president and 50 for Miss America?

15. Isn't having a smoking section in a restaurant like having a peeing section in a swimming pool?

16. Why is it that most nudists are people you don't want to see naked?

17. Snowmen fall from Heaven unassembled.

18. Every time I walk into a singles bar I can hear Mom's wise words: "Don't pick that up, you don't know where it's been!"

Subject: GREAT SIGNS

On a Septic Tank Truck in Oregon:
"Yesterday's Meals on Wheels"

On a Septic Tank Truck sign:
"We're #1 in the #2 business."

Sign over a Gynecologist's Office:
"Dr. Jones, at your cervix."

At a Proctologist's door
"To expedite your visit please back in."

On a Plumber's truck:
"We repair what your husband fixed."

On a Plumber's truck:
"Don't sleep with a drip. Call your plumber."

Pizza Shop Slogan:
"7 days without pizza makes one weak."

At a Tire Shop in Milwaukee:
"Invite us to your next blowout."

On a Plastic Surgeon's Office door:
"Hello. Can we pick your nose?"

At A Towing company:
"We don't charge an arm and a leg. We want tows."

In a Restaurant window:
"Don't stand there and be hungry, Come on in and get fed up."

In the front yard of a Funeral Home:
"Drive carefully. We'll wait."

At a Propane Filling Station,
"Thank heaven for little grills."

On An Electrician's truck:
"Let us remove your shorts."

In a Nonsmoking Area:
"If we see smoke, we will assume you are on fire and take appropriate action."

On A Maternity Room door:
"Push. Push. Push."

At an Optometrist's Office
"If you don't see what you're looking for, you've come to the right place."

On a Taxidermist's window:
"We really know our stuff."

In a Podiatrist's office:
"Time wounds all heels."

On a Fence:
"Salesmen welcome! Dog food is expensive."

At a Car Dealership:
"The best way to get back on your feet – miss a car payment."

Outside a Muffler Shop:
"No appointment necessary. We hear you coming."

In a Veterinarian's waiting room:
"Be back in 5 minutes. Sit! Stay!

At the Electric company:
"We would be delighted if you send in your payment. However, if you don't, you will be."

Some people try to turn back their odometers. Not me, I want people to know "why" I look this way. I've traveled a long way and some of the roads weren't paved.

How old would you be if you didn't know how old you are?

When you are dissatisfied and would like to go back to youth, think of Algebra.

You know you are getting old when everything either dries up or leaks.

I don't know how I got over the hill without getting to the top.

One of the many things no one tells you about aging is that it is such a nice change from being young.

Ah, being young is beautiful, but being old is comfortable.

Old age is when former classmates are so gray and wrinkled and bald, they don't recognize you.

If you don't learn to laugh at trouble, you won't have anything to laugh at when you are old.

First you forget names, then you forget faces. Then you forget to pull up your zipper. It's worse when you forget to pull it down.

Long ago when men cursed and beat the ground with sticks, it was called witchcraft.. Today, it's called golf

A WELL PLANNED LIFE????

Two women met for the first time since graduating from high school. One asked the other, "You were always so organized in school, Did you manage to live a well planned life?"

"Yes," said her friend. "My first marriage was to a millionaire; my second marriage to an actor; my third marriage was to a preacher; and now I'm married to an undertaker."

Her friend asked, "What do those marriages have to do with a well planned life?"

"One for the money, two for the show, three to get ready, and four to go."

New Rules!

Dear Employee:

As a result of the reduction of money budgeted for certain areas, we are forced to cut down on our number of personnel. Under this plan, older employees will be asked to take early retirement, thus permitting the retention of younger people who represent our future. Therefore, a program to phase out older personnel by the end of the current fiscal year, via retirement, will be placed into effect immediately. This program will be known as SLAP (Sever Late-Aged Personnel). Employees who are SLAPPED will be given the opportunity to look for jobs outside the company. SLAPPED employees can request a review of their employment records before actual retirement takes place. This review phase of the program is called SCREW. SCREW (Survey of Capabilities of Retired Early Workers). All employees who have been SLAPPED and SCREWED may file an appeal with upper management. This appeal is called SHAFT (Study by Higher Authority Following Termination). Under the terms of the new policy, an employee may be SLAPPED once, SCREWED twice, but may be SHAFTED as many times as the company deems appropriate. If an employee follows the above procedure, he/she will be entitled to get:

HERPES (Half Earnings for Retired Personnel's Early Severance) or CLAP (Combined Lump sum Assistance Payment).

Employees with HERPES or CLAP will no longer be SLAPPED, or SCREWED by the company. Management wishes to assure the younger employees who remain on board that the company will continue its policy of training employees through our: Special High Intensity Training (SHIT). We take pride in the amount of SHIT our employees receive. We have given our employees more SHIT than any company in this area. If any employee feels they do not receive enough SHIT on the job, see your immediate supervisor. Your supervisor is specially trained to make sure you receive all the SHIT you can stand. And, once again, thanks for all your years of service with us.

The value of the yen

An Asian man walked into the currency exchange in New York with 2000 yen and walked out with $72. The following week, he walked in with 2000 yen and was handed $66. He asked the teller why he got less money than he had gotten the previous week. The lady answers, "Fluctuations." As he stormed out the door, he yelled out… "Fluc you Amelicans too"

Q. What's the height of conceit?
A. Having an orgasm and calling out your own name.

Q. What's the definition of macho?
A. Jogging home from your own vasectomy.

Q. What's the difference between a G-Spot and a golf ball?
A. A guy will actually search for a golf ball.

Q. Why is divorce so expensive?
A. Because it's worth it.

Q. What is a Yankee?
A. The same as a quickie, but a guy can do it alone.

Q. What do Tupperware and a walrus have in common?
A. They both like a tight seal.

Q. What is the difference between "ooooooh" and "aaaaaah"?
A. About three inches.

Q. What do you call a lesbian with fat fingers?
A. Well-hung.

Q. What's the difference between purple and pink?
A. The grip.

Q. How do you find a Blind Man in a nudist colony?
A. It's not hard.

Q. How do you circumcise a hillbilly?
A. Kick his sister in the jaw.

Q. What's the difference between a girlfriend and a wife?
A. 150 lbs.

Q. What's the difference between a boyfriend and a husband?
A. 45 minutes

Q. Why do men find it difficult to make eye contact?
A. Breasts don't have eyes.

Q: If the dove is the bird of peace, what is the bird of true love?
A: The swallow.

Q: What is the difference between medium and rare?
A. Six inches is medium, eight inches is rare.

Q. Why do most women pay more attention to their appearance than improving their minds?
A. Because most men are stupid but few are blind.

Q. Why do women rub their eyes when they get up in the morning?
A. They don't have balls to scratch.

(Q) Why do men want to marry virgins?
(A) They can't stand criticism.

(Q) Why is it so hard for women to find men that are sensitive, caring, and good looking?
(A) Because those men already have boyfriends.

(Q) What's the difference between a new husband and a new dog?
(A) After a year, the dog is still excited to see you.

(Q) What makes men chase women they have no intention of marrying?
(A) The same urge that makes dogs chase cars they have no intention of driving.

(Q) What do you call a smart blonde?
(A) A golden retriever.

(Q) Why does the bride always wear white?
(A) Because it's good for the dishwasher to match the stove and refrigerator.

(Q) A brunette, a blonde, and a redhead are all in third grade. Who has the biggest boobs?
(A) The blonde, because she's 18.

(Q) Which sexual position produces the ugliest children?
(A) Ask your Mom.

(Q) What is the quickest way to clear out a men's restroom?
(A) Say, "Nice Dick."

(Q) Why don't bunnies make noise when they have sex?
(A) Because they have cotton balls.

(Q) What did the blonde say when she found out she was pregnant?
(A) "Are you sure it's mine?"

(Q) What's the difference between Beer Nuts and Deer Nuts?
(A) Beer Nuts are under $1, and Deer Nuts are always under a buck.

(Q) What would you call it when an Italian has one arm shorter than the other?
(A) A speech impediment.

Did you hear about the dyslexic Rabbi? He walks around saying "Yo."

(Q) What's the difference between a Southern zoo, and a Northern zoo?
(A) A Southern zoo has a description of the animal on the front of the cage, along with a recipe.

(Q) What's the Cuban National Anthem?
(A) Row, row, row your boat.

(Q) What's the difference between a Northern fairytale and a Southern fairytale?
(A) A Northern fairytale begins "Once upon a time." A Southern fairytale begins "Y'all ain't gonna believe this s—t."

(Q) What's the best form of birth control after 50?
(A) Nudity.

(Q) How many women does it take to change a light bulb?
(A) None, they just sit there in the dark and bitch.

(Q) What's the fastest way to a man's heart?
(A) Through his chest with a sharp knife.

(Q) Why are men and parking spaces alike?
(A) Because all the good ones are taken and the only ones left are disabled.

HAIRDO

An old man was sitting on a bench at the mall. A teenager walked up to the bench and sat down. He had spiked hair in all different colours: green, red, orange, blue and yellow. The old man was staring. The teenager finally said sarcastically, "What's the matter old timer, never done anything wild in your life?" Without batting an eye, the old man replied, "Got drunk once and had sex with a peacock. I was just wondering if you were my son."

MEDICAL RESEARCH

There is more money being spent on breast implants and Viagra, and related products, today than on Alzheimer's research. This means that by 2040 there should be a large elderly population with perky breasts, and huge erections, and absolutely no recollection of what to do with them.

THE BIRDS AND THE BEES

Cyrus says: "Daddy, how was I born?"
Dad says: "Ah, my son, I guess one day you will need to find out anyway! Well, you see your Mom and I first got together in a chat room on MSN. Then I set up a date via e-mail with your mom and we met at a cyber-café.

We sneaked into a secluded room, where your mother agreed to a download from my hard drive. As soon as I was ready to upload, we discovered that neither one of us had used a firewall, and since it was too late to hit the delete button, nine months later a blessed little Pop-Up appeared and said: You've Got Male! And that's the story, Virus...I mean Cyrus."

MISS BEA

Miss Bea, the church organist, was in her eighties and had never been married. She was much admired for her sweetness and kindness to all.

The pastor came to call on her one afternoon early in the spring, and she welcomed him into her Victorian parlor. She invited him to have a seat while she prepared a little tea.

As he sat facing her old pump organ, the young minister noticed a cut glass bowl sitting on top of it, filled with water. In the water floated, of all things, a condom. Imagine his shock and surprise. Imagine his curiosity! Surely Miss Bea had flipped or something...!

When she returned with tea and cookies, they began to chat. The pastor tried to stifle his curiosity about the bowl of water and its strange floater, but soon it got the better of him, and he could resist no longer. "Miss Bea," he said, "I wonder if you would tell me about this?" (pointing to the bowl).

"Oh, yes," she replied, "isn't it wonderful? I was walking downtown last fall and I found this little package on the ground. The directions said to put it on the organ, keep it wet, and it would prevent disease. And you know...I haven't had a cold all winter."

MEN AND WOMEN

The ladies will like this as it finally all makes sense now:

MENtal illness

MENstrual cramps

MENtal breakdown

MENopause

GUYnocologist

AND...

When we have REAL trouble, it's a HISterectomy.

Notice how all of women's problems start with MEN?

One evening a preschooler, Hannah, and her parents Alan and Robin were sitting on the couch chatting. Hannah asked, "Daddy, you're the boss of the house, right?"

Alan proudly replied, "Yes, I am the boss of the house."

But Hannah quickly burst his bubble when she added, "Cause Mommy put you in charge, huh, Daddy?"

LOST IN TRANSLATION

Two Mexican detectives were investigating the murder of Juan Gonzalez. "How was he killed?" asked one detective. "With a golf gun," the other detective replied. "A golf gun?! What is a golf gun?" "I don't know. But it sure made a hole in Juan."

This guy has been sitting in a bar all night, staring at a blonde wearing the tightest pants he's ever seen. Finally, his curiosity gets the best of him, so he walks over and asks, "How do you get into those pants?" The young woman looks him over and replies, "Well, you could start by buying me a drink."

Moe: "My wife got me to believe in religion." Joe: "Really?" Moe: "Yeah. Until I married her I didn't believe in hell."

A man is recovering from surgery when a nurse asks him how he is feeling. "I'm O.K. but I didn't like the four-letter-word the doctor used in surgery," he answered. "What did he say," asked the nurse. "OOPS!"

While shopping for vacation clothes, my husband and I passed a display of bathing suits. It had been at least ten years and twenty pounds since I had even considered buying a bathing suit, so I sought my husband's advice. "What do you think?" I asked. "Should I get a bikini or an all-in-one?" "Better get a bikini," he replied. "You'd never get it all in one."

Grandpa was driving with his 9 year old granddaughter and beeped the horn by mistake. She turned and looked at him for an explanation. He said, "I did that by accident." She replied, "I know that, Grandpa." He replied, "How did you know?" She said, "Because you didn't say "a-----e" afterwards."

Holiday Party

December 1

TO: ALL EMPLOYEES

I'm happy to inform you that the company Christmas Party will take place on December 23rd at Luigi's Open Pit Barbecue. There will be lots of spiked eggnog and a small band playing traditional carols...feel free to sing along. And don't be surprised if our CEO shows up dressed as Santa Claus to light the Christmas tree!

Exchange of gifts among employees can be done at that time; however, no gift should be over $10. Merry Christmas to you and your family.

Patty Lewis

Human Resources Director

December 2nd

TO: ALL EMPLOYEES

In no way was yesterday's memo intended to exclude our Jewish employees. We recognize that, Hanukkah is an important holiday that often coincides with Christmas (though unfortunately not this year).

However, from now on we're calling it our "Holiday Party." The same policy applies to employees who are celebrating Kwanzaa at this time. There will be no Christmas tree and no Christmas carols sung.

Happy Holidays to you and your family.

Patty Lewis

Human Resources Director

December 3rd

TO: ALL EMPLOYEES

Regarding the anonymous note I received from a member of
Alcoholics Anonymous requesting a non-drinking table, I'm happy
to accommodate this request, but, don't forget, if I put a sign on the
table that reads, "AA Only," you won't be anonymous anymore. In
addition, forget about the gifts exchange-no gifts will be allowed
since the union members feel that $10 is too much money.

Patty Lewis

Human Resources Director

December 7th

TO: ALL EMPLOYEES

I've arranged for members of Overeaters Anonymous to sit
farthest from the dessert buffet and pregnant women closest to the
restrooms. Gays are allowed to sit with each other. Lesbians do
not have to sit with the gay men; each will have their table. Yes,
there will be a flower arrangement for the gay men's table. Happy
now?

Patty Lewis

Human Resources Director

December 9th

TO: ALL EMPLOYEES

People, people-nothing sinister was intended by wanting our CEO
to play Santa Claus! Even if the anagram of "Santa" does happen
to be "Satan," there is no evil connotation to our own "little man in
a red suit."

Patty Lewis

Human Resources Director

December 10th

TO: ALL EMPLOYEES

Vegetarians-I've had it with you people!! We're going to hold this party at Luigi's Open Pit whether you like it or not, you can just sit at the table farthest from the "grill of death," as you put it, and you'll get salad bar only, including hydroponic tomatoes. But, you know, tomatoes have feelings, too. They scream when you slice them. I've heard them scream. I'm hearing them right now...Ha! I hope you all have a rotten holiday?

Drive drunk and die, you hear me?

The Bitch from Hell

December 14th

TO: ALL EMPLOYEES

I'm sure I speak for all of us in wishing Patty Lewis a speedy recovery form her stress-related illness. I'll continue to forward your cards to her at the sanitarium. In the meantime, management has decided to cancel our Holiday Party and give everyone the afternoon of the 23rd off with full pay.

Happy Holidays!

Terri Bishop

Acting Human Resources Director

This Russian aristocrat and this newly rich Russian were both in the bathroom of this very fine restaurant at the urinals, standing side by side. The newly rich Russian says to the aristocrat, "Russia is truly a marvelous country. You have a big car, I have a big car. You want to go to an expensive restaurant, you can go. I want to go to an expensive restaurant, I can go. You want to wear a fine fur coat, you can as I can, and we both are wearing one right now. But, I have one question. When I urinate, it makes a rushing, noisy and strong sound like the Volga, but when you urinate it makes a sound, quiet like the Don. Why?" The aristocrat answers, "Peasant, I'm pissing on your fur coat."

Can you guess which of the following are true and which are false?

1. Apples, not caffeine, are more efficient at waking you up in the morning.

2. A pack-a-day smoker will lose approximately 2 teeth every 10 years.

3. People do not get sick from cold weather; it's from being indoors a lot more.

4. When you sneeze, all bodily functions stop, even your heart!

5. Only 7 per cent of the population are lefties.

6. Forty people are sent to the hospital for dog bites every minute.

7. Babies are born without kneecaps. They don't appear until they are 2-6 years old.

8. The average person over 50 will have spent 5 years waiting in lines.

9. The toothbrush was invented in 1498.

10. The average housefly lives for one month.

11. 40,000 Americans are injured by toilets each year.

12. A coat hanger is 44 inches long when straightened.

13. The average computer user blinks 7 times a minute.

14. Your feet are bigger in the afternoon than any other time of day

15. Most of us have eaten a spider in our sleep.

16. The REAL reason ostriches stick their head in the sand is to search for water.

17. The only two animals that can see behind themselves without turning their heads are the rabbit and the parrot.

18. John Travolta turned down the starring roles in "An Officer and a Gentleman": and "Tootsie."

19. Michael Jackson owns the rights to the South Carolina State anthem.

20. In most television commercials advertising milk, a mixture of white paint and a little thinner is used in place of the milk.

21. Prince Charles and Prince William NEVER travel on the same airplane, just in case there is a crash.

22. The first Harley Davidson motorcycle built in 1903 used a tomato can for a carburetor.

23. Most hospitals make money by selling the umbilical cords cut from women who give birth. They are used in vein transplant surgery.

24. Humphrey Bogart was related to Princess Diana. They were 7th cousins.

25. If coloring weren't added to Coca-Cola, it would be green.

They are all true.......Now go back and think about #15.

An American golfer playing in Ireland hooked his drive into the woods. Looking for his ball, he found a little Leprechaun flat on his back, a big bump on his head and the golfer's ball beside him.

Horrified, the American golfer got his water bottle from the cart and poured it over the little guy, reviving him.

"Arrgh! What happened?" the Leprechaun asked. "Oh, I see. Well, ye got me fair and square. Ye get three wishes, so whaddya want?"

"Thank God, you're all right!" the golfer answered in relief. "I don't want anything. I'm just glad you're OK, and I apologize. I really didn't mean to hit you." And the golfer walked off.

"What a nice guy," the Leprechaun said to himself. "But it was fair and square that he got me, and I have to do something for him. I'll give him the three things I would want....a great golf game, all the money he ever needs, and a fantastic sex life."

A year went by (as it does in stories like this) and the same American golfer returned to Ireland. On the same hole, he again hit a bad drive into the woods and the Leprechaun was there waiting for him. "Twas me that made ye hit the ball here," the little guy said. "I just want to ask ye, how's yer golf game?"

"My game is fantastic!" the golfer answered. "In fact, that's the first bad ball I've hit in a year! I'm an internationally famous golfer now." He added, "By the way, it's good to see you're all right."

"Oh, I'm fine now thankee. I did that fer yer golf game, you know. And tell me, how's yer money situation?"

"Why, it's just wonderful!" the golfer stated. "I win fortunes in golf. if I need cash, I just reach in my pocket and pull out $100.00 bills I didn't even know were there!"

"I did that fer ye also. And tell me, how's yer sex life?"

The golfer blushed, turned his head away in embarrassment, and said shyly, "It's OK."

"C'mon, c'mon, now," urged the Leprechaun, "I'm wanting to know if I did a good job. How many times a day?"

Blushing even more, the golfer looked around then whispered, "Once—sometimes twice a week."

"What??" responded the Leprechaun in shock. "That's all? Only once or twice a week?"

"Well, said the golfer, "I figure that's not bad for a Catholic priest in a small town!"

Blond GUY joke….

An Irishman, a Mexican and a Blond Guy were doing construction work on scaffolding on the 20th floor of a building. They were eating lunch and the Irishman said, "Corned beef and cabbage! If I get corned beef and cabbage one more time for lunch, I'm going to jump off this building."

The Mexican opened his lunch box and exclaimed, "Burritos again! If I get burritos one more time I'm going to jump off, too."

The blond opened his lunch and said, "Bologna again! If I get a bologna sandwich one more time, I'm jumping too."

The next day, the Irishman opened his lunch box, saw corned beef and cabbage, and jumped to his death. The Mexican opened his lunch, saw a burrito, and jumped, too. The blond guy opened his lunch, saw the bologna sandwich and jumped to his death as well.

At the funeral, the Irishman's wife was weeping. She said, "If I'd known how really tired he was of corned beef and cabbage, I never would have given it to him again!"

The Mexican's wife also wept and said, "I could have given him tacos or enchiladas! I didn't realize he hated burritos so much."

Everyone turned and stared at the blond's wife. The blonde's wife said, "Don' t look at me. He makes his own lunch!"

A wife arrived home from a shopping trip and was shocked to find her husband in bed with a lovely young woman. Just as she was about to storm out of the house, her husband called out; "Perhaps you should hear how all this came about..." "I was driving home on the highway when I saw this young woman looking tired and bedraggled. I brought her home and made her a meal from the roast beef you had forgotten about in the fridge. She was bare-footed, so I gave her your good sandals which you had discarded because they had gone out of style."

"She was cold, so I gave her the sweater which I bought for you for your birthday, but you never wore because the color didn't suit you. Her pants were torn, so I gave her a pair of your jeans, which were perfectly good, but are too small for you now." "Then just as she was about to leave, she asked me, "Is there...anything else your wife doesn't use anymore?"

"That wife of mine is a liar," said the angry husband to a sympathetic pal seated next to him at the bar. "How do you know?" the friend asked. "She didn't come home last night, and when I asked her where she'd been, she said that she had spent the night with her sister, Shirley." "So?" "So she's a liar. I spent the night with her sister, Shirley."

Valentine Greetings From A Curmudgeon?

These are entries to a competition where a first line is the MOST
romantic, and the second line is the LEAST.

Love may be beautiful, love may be bliss
but I only slept with you, 'cause I was pissed

Roses are red, violets are blue,
Sugar is sweet, and so are you.   '
But the roses are wilting, the violets are dead,
The sugar bowl's empty and so is your head.

With loving beauty you float with grace
If only you could hide your face

Kind, intelligent, loving and hot
This describes everything you're not

I love your smile, your face, your eyes
Damn, I'm good at telling lies!

My darling, my lover, my beautiful wife,
Marrying you screwed up my life

I want to feel your sweet and tender embrace
Just don't remove the paper bag from your face

I see your face when I am dreaming
That's why I always wake up screaming

My love, you take my breath away
What have you stepped in to smell this way

What inspired this amorous rhyme?
Two parts vodka, one part lime

One day out in the Texas panhandle, a guy sees a sign in front of a house: "Talking Dog for Sale." He rings the bell and the owner tells him the dog is in the backyard. The guy goes into the backyard and sees a black Lab just sitting there. "You talk?" he asks. "Yep," the Lab replies. "So, what's your story?" The lab looks up and says, "Well, I discovered this gift pretty young and I wanted to help the government, so I told the CIA about my gift, and in no time they had me jetting from country to country, sitting in rooms with spies and world leaders, because no one figured a dog would be eavesdropping. I was one of their most valuable spies eight years running.".

"The jetting around really tired me out, and I knew I wasn't getting any younger and I wanted to settle down. So I signed up for a job at the airport to do some undercover security work, mostly wandering near suspicious characters and listening in. I uncovered some incredible dealings there and was awarded a batch of medals. Had a wife, a mess of puppies, and now I'm just retired." The guy is amazed. He goes back in and asks the owner what he wants for the dog. "Ten dollars." The guy says, "This dog is amazing. Why on earth are you selling him so cheap?" "He's a liar. He didn't do any of that stuff."

The girl was supposed to write a short story in as few words as possible for her college class and the instructions were that it had to discuss Religion, Sexuality and Mystery. She was the only one who received an A+ and this is what she wrote: Good God, I'm pregnant, I wonder who did it.

Dave works hard at the plant and spends most evening bowling or playing basketball at the gym. His wife thinks he is pushing himself too hard, so for his birthday she takes him to a local strip club. The doorman at the club greets them and says, "Hey, Dave! How ya doin?" His wife is puzzled and asks if he's been to this club before. "Oh no," says Dave. "He's on my bowling team." When they are seated, a waitress asks Dave if he'd like his usual and brings over a Budweiser. His wife is becoming increasingly uncomfortable and says, "How did she know that you drink Budweiser?" "She's in the Ladies' Bowling League, honey. We share lanes with them."

A stripper then comes over to their table, throws her arms around Dave, starts to rub herself all over him and says "Hi, Davey. Want your usual table dance, big boy?" Dave's wife, now furious, grabs her purse and storms out of the club. Dave follows and spots her getting into a cab. Before she can slam the door, he jumps in beside her. Dave tries desperately to explain how the stripper must have mistaken him for someone else, but his wife is having none of it. She is screaming at him at the top of her lungs, calling him every 4 letter word in the book. The cabby turns his head and says, "Looks like you picked up a real bitch tonight, Dave."

Little Red Riding Hood is skipping down the road when she sees a big bad wolf crouched down behind a log. "My, what big eyes you have, Mr. Wolf." The wolf jumps up and runs away. Further down the road Little Red Riding Hood sees the wolf again and this time he is crouched behind a bush. "My what big ears you have, Mr. Wolf." Again the wolf jumps up and runs away. About two miles down the road Little Red Riding Hood sees the wolf again and this time he is crouched down behind a rock. "My what big teeth you have, Mr. Wolf." With that the wolf jumps up and screams, "Will you go away? I'm trying to poop!"

A rich Beverly Hills woman got very angry at her maid. After a long list of stinging remarks about her shortcomings as a cook and housekeeper, she dismissed the maid. The maid couldn't allow such abuse to go unanswered. "Your husband considers me a better housekeeper and cook than you, Madam. He has told me himself." "I suppose my husband told you that?" "Yes, he did. And furthermore," the angry maid continued, "I am better in bed than you!" "And I suppose my husband told you that, too?" "No, Madam," said the maid. "The mailman did."

An 85-year old gentleman marries a gorgeous 20-year old babe.
On the wedding night they're in his mansion, it's bedtime and the
wife escorts the gentleman to his own bedroom explaining in a
gentle way that she is concerned about his health, namely, that he
should not be exerting himself excessively. A short while later,
there is a tap-tap on the wife's bedroom door. The husband enters,
they're in bed, and he is in top form. Afterward, he returns to
his bedroom. An hour later, there is another tap-tap on the wife's
bedroom door, and sure enough the husband has shown up for
round two. And he is really on top of his game. Afterward he
returns to his own quarters. An hour later, there is a tap-tap a third
time. This time, the guy carries on in ways unimaginable to his
very impressed wife. Afterward before making his exit, the wife
asks the husband, "How were you able to perform so wonderfully
three times?" To which the husband replies, "You mean this wasn't
my first visit?"

Kids were asked questions about the Old and New Testaments. The following statements about the Bible were written by children. They have not been retouched or corrected (i.e., incorrect spelling has been left in).

1. In the first book of the bible, Guinessis, God got tired of creating the world, so he took the Sabbath off.

2. Adam and Eve were created from an apple tree. Noah's wife was called Joan of Ark. Noah built an ark, which the animals come on to in pears.

3. Lot's wife was a pillar of salt by day, but a ball of fire by night.

4. The Jews were a proud people and throughout history they had trouble with the unsympathetic Genitals.

5. Samson was a strongman who let himself be led astray by a Jezebel like Delilah.

6. Samson slayed the Philistines with the axe of the Apostles.

7. Moses led the Hebrews to the Red Sea, where they made unleavened bread which is bread without any ingredients.

8. The Egyptians were all drowned in the dessert. Afterwards, Moses went up on Mount Cyanide to get the ten amendments.

9. The first commandment was when Eve told Adam to eat the apple

10. The seventh commandment is thou shalt not admit adultery.

11. Moses died before he ever reached Canada. Then Joshua led the Hebrews in the battle of Geritol.

12. The greatest miracle in the Bible is when Joshua told his son to stand still and he obeyed him

13. David was a Hebrew king skilled at playing the liar. He fought the Finklesteins, a race of people who lived in Biblical times.

14. Solomon, one of David's sons, had 300 wives and 700 porcupines.

15. When the three wise guys from the East Side arrived, they found Jesus in the manager.

16. The people who followed the lord were called the 12 decibels.

17. The epistles were the wives of the apostles.

18. One of the oppossums was St. Matthew who was also a taximan.

19. St. Paul cavorted to Christianity. He preached holy acrimony, which is another name for marriage.

20. Christians have only one spouse. This is called monotony

VIRUSES TO LOOK OUT FOR

THE GEORGE W. BUSH VIRUS: Causes your computer to pretend it can think.

THE BILL CLINTON VIRUS: Gives you a 7 Inch Hard Drive with No memory.

THE BOB DOLE (AKA: VIAGRA) VIRUS: Makes a new hard drive out of an old floppy.

THE AL GORE VIRUS: Causes your computer to just keep counting.

THE MONICA LEWINSKY VIRUS: Sucks all the memory out of your computer, then emails everyone about what it did.

THE JESSE JACKSON VIRUS: Warns you constantly about illegitimate reproduction, while illegitimately reproducing files in the background.

THE MIKE TYSON VIRUS: Quits after two bytes.

THE JACK KEVORKIAN VIRUS: Deletes all old files.

THE PROZAC VIRUS: Totally screws up your RAM, but your processor doesn't care.

THE JOEY BUTTAFUOCO VIRUS: Only attacks minor files.

THE ARNOLD SCHWARZENEGGER VIRUS: Terminates some files, leaves, but will be back.

THE LORENA BOBBITT VIRUS: Reformats your hard drive into a 3.5-inch floppy, then discards it through Windows.

A bear walks into a bar in Billings, Montana and sits down. He bangs on the bar with his paw and demands a beer. The bartender approaches and says, "We don't serve beer to bears in bars in Billings." The bear, becoming angry, demands again that he be served a beer. The bartender tells him again, more forcefully, "We don't serve beer to belligerent bears in bars in Billings."

The bear, very angry now, says, "If you don't serve me a beer, I'm going to eat that lady sitting at the end of the bar." The bartender says, "Sorry, we don't serve beer to belligerent, bully bears in bars in Billings." The bear goes to the end of the bar, and, as promised, eats the woman. He comes back to his seat and again demands a beer. The bartender states, "Sorry, we don't serve beer to belligerent, bully bears in bars in Billings who are on drugs." The bear says, "I'm NOT on drugs." The bartender says, "You are now. That was a barbitchyouate."

Little Henry is on the beach with his parents when he says to his mother, "Mommy, can I go swimming in the sea?" "No," she replies, "the water is too deep and too rough for you." "But daddy has just gone in," says Henry. "I know, darling, but your daddy's insured."

An old man, Mr. Smith, resided in a nursing home. One day he went into the nurses office and informed Nurse Jones that his penis had died. She realized that he was old and forgetful and decided to humor him, "It did? I'm sorry to hear that", she replied. Two days later Mr. Smith was walking down the halls of the nursing home with his penis hanging outside of his pants. Nurse Jones saw him and said, "Mr. Smith! I thought you said your penis died!?" "It did", he replied, "Today's the viewing!"

SECURITY SEX

Two men were talking. So, how's your sex life?" "Oh, nothing special. I'm having Social Security sex." "Social Security sex?" "Yeah, you know: I get a little each month, but not enough to live on."

LOUD SEX:

A wife went in to see a therapist and said, "I've got a big problem, doctor. Every time we're in bed and my husband climaxes, he lets out this ear splitting yell." "My dear," the shrink said, "that's completely natural. I don't see what the problem is." "The problem is," she complained, "It wakes me up."

CONFOUNDED SEX

A man was in a terrible accident, and his "manhood" was mangled and torn from his body. His doctor assured him that modern medicine could give him back his manhood, but that his insurance wouldn't cover the surgery since it was considered cosmetic The doctor said the cost would be $3,500 for "small", $6,500 for "medium", $14,000 for "large." The man was sure he would want a medium or large, but the doctor urged him to talk it over with his wife before he made any decision. The man called his wife on the phone and explained their options. The doctor came back into the room, and found the man looking dejected. "Well, what have the two of you decided?" asked the doctor. The man answered, "She'd rather remodel the kitchen".

WEDDING ANNIVERSARY SEX

A husband and his wife had a bitter quarrel on the day of their 40th wedding anniversary. The husband yells, "When you die, I'm getting you a headstone that reads: 'Here Lies My Wife – Cold As Ever'." "Yeah," she replied, "And when you die, I'm getting you a headstone that reads: Here Lies My Husband – Stiff At Last.'"

WOMEN'S HUMOR

My husband came home with a tube of KY jelly and said, "This will make you happy tonight. He was right. When he went out of the bedroom, I squirted it all over the doorknobs. He couldn't get back in."

AND LASTLY......

One night an 87 yr old woman came home from Bingo to find her 92 yr old husband in bed with another woman. She became violent and ended up pushing him off the balcony of their 20th floor assisted living apartment...killing him instantly. Brought before the court on charge of murder, the judge asked her if she had anything to say in her defense. She began coolly, "Yes, your honor. I figured that at 92, if he could have sex, he could fly."

THE SKI TRIP

Jack decided to go skiing with his buddy, Bob. So they loaded up Jack's mini van and headed north. After driving for a few hours, they got caught in a terrible blizzard. So they pulled into a nearby farm and asked the attractive lady who answered the door if they could spend the night. "I realize it's terrible weather out there and I have this huge house all to myself, but I'm recently widowed," she explained. "I'm afraid the neighbors will talk if I let you stay in my house."

"Don't worry," Jack said. "We'll be happy to sleep in the barn. And if the weather breaks, we'll be gone at first light." The lady agreed, and the two men found their way to the barn and settled in for the night. Come morning, the weather had cleared, and they got on their way. They enjoyed a great weekend of skiing. But about nine months later, Jack got an unexpected letter from an attorney. It took him a few minutes to figure it out, but he finally determined that it was from the attorney of that attractive widow he had met on the ski weekend. He dropped in on his friend Bob and asked, "Bob, do you remember that good-looking widow from the farm we stayed at on out ski holiday up North about 9 months ago?"

"Yes, I do," said Bob "Did you, er, happen to get up in the middle of the night, go up to the house and pay her a visit?" "Well, um, yes," Bob said, a little embarrassed about being found out. "I have to admit that I did." "And did you happen to use my name instead of telling her your name?" Bob's face turned beet red and he said, "Yeah, look, I'm sorry, buddy. I'm afraid I did. Why do you ask?" "She just died and left me everything."

One Sunday evening, Harvey and Gladys are getting ready for bed. Gladys is standing in front of her full-length mirror, taking a long, hard look at herself. "You know, Harvey," she comments. "I stare into this mirror and I see an ancient creature. My face is all wrinkled, my arms and legs are as flabby as popped balloons, and my butt looks like a sad, deflated version of the Hindenberg!" She turns to face her husband and says, "Dear, please tell me just one positive thing about my body so I can feel better about myself." Harvey studies Gladys critically for a moment and then says in a soft, thoughtful voice, "Well…there's nothing wrong with your eyesight." Services for Harvey's funeral will be held Tuesday morning at 10:30.

A cabbie picks up a nun. She gets into the cab, and the cab driver won't stop staring at her. She asks him why is he staring and he replies, "I have a question to ask you, but I don't want to offend you." She answers, "My dear son, you cannot offend me. When you're as old as I am and have been a nun as long as I have, you get a chance to see and hear just about everything. I'm sure that there's nothing you could say or ask that I would find offensive." "Well, I've always had a fantasy to have a nun kiss me." She responds, "Well, let's see what we can do about that: #1, you have to be single and #2, you must be Catholic." The cab driver is very excited and says, "Yes, I am single and I'm Catholic too!" "OK" the nun says "Pull into the next alley" He does and the nun fulfills his fantasy with a kiss that would make a hooker blush. But when they get back on the road, the cab driver starts crying. "My dear child," said the nun, "Why are you crying?" "Forgive me sister, but I have sinned. I lied, I must confess, I'm married and I'm not Catholic." The nun says, "That's OK, my name is Kevin and I'm on my way to a Halloween party!"

THE NOTE

A mother passing by her daughter's bedroom was astonished to see the bed was nicely made and everything was picked up. Then she saw an envelope propped up prominently on the center of the bed. It was addressed, "Mom." With the worst premonition, she opened the envelope and read the letter with trembling hands:

Dear Mom,

It is with great regret and sorrow that I'm writing you. I had to elope with my new boyfriend because I wanted to avoid a scene with Dad and you. I've been finding real passion with John and he is so nice – even with all his piercing, tattoos, beard, and his motorcycle clothes. But it's not only the passion mom, I'm pregnant, and John said that we will be very happy. He already owns a trailer in the woods and has a stack of firewood for the whole winter. He wants to have many more children with me and that's now one of my dreams too.

John taught me that marijuana doesn't really hurt anyone and we'll be growing it for us and trading it with his friends for all the cocaine and ecstasy we want. In the meantime, we'll pray that science will find a cure for AIDS, so John can get better; he sure deserves it!! Don't worry Mom, I'm 15 years old now and I know how to take care of myself. Some day I'm sure we'll be back to visit so you can get to know your grandchildren. Your daughter, Julie

PS: Mom, none of the above is true. I'm over at the next-door neighbor's house. I just wanted to remind you that there are worse things in life than my report card which is in my desk drawer. I love you! Call when it is safe for me to come home.

A woman walks into a pharmacy and asked the pharmacist for some arsenic. He asks "What for?" She says "I want to kill my husband". He says "Sorry, I can't do that." She then reaches into her handbag and pulls out a photo of her husband in bed with the pharmacist's wife and hands it to him. He says, "You didn't tell me you had a prescription..."

An elderly man goes to his doctor complaining of aches and pains all over his body. After a thorough examination the doctor give him a clean bill of health. "You're in excellent shape for an 85 year old man. But I'm not a magician – I can't make you any younger", says the doctor. "Who asked you to make me younger?" says Max. "Just make sure I get older!"

This guy spends his time in the service in Japan. He meets and marries this beautiful Japanese woman. They return to the USA when his service is done. Only problem is that she can't speak English. But she is very inventive and figures out a way around this. One day she is shopping in this butcher shop and she wants some chicken thighs, so she lifts her skirt and points to her thighs. The butcher understands and gives her some chicken thighs. The next day she wants to get some chicken breasts, so when she is at the butcher shop she raises her sweater and points to her breast. The butcher understands and gives her some chicken breasts. The following day she wants to get some sausage. So she brings her husband with her when she goes shopping. Do you know why she brings her husband with her? A-Because he could speak English.

Miriam was dying and on her deathbed, she gave final instructions to her husband Sidney. "Sidney, you've been so good to me all these years. I know you never even thought about another woman. But now that I'm going, I want you to marry again as soon as possible and I want you to give your new wife all my expensive clothes." "I can't do that, darling," Sidney said. "You're a size 16 and she's only a 10."

8 WORDS WITH TWO MEANINGS

1. THINGY (thing-ee) n. Female......Any part under a car's hood. Male.....The strap fastener on a woman's bra.

2. VULNERABLE (vul-ne-ra-bel) adj. Female....Fully opening up one's self emotionally to another. Male....Playing football without a cup.

3. COMMUNICATION (ko-myoo-ni-kay-shon) n. Female...The open sharing of thoughts and feelings with one's partner. Male... Leaving a note before taking off on a fishing trip with the boys.

4. COMMITMENT (ko-mit-ment) n. Female....A desire to get married and raise a family. Male.....Trying not to hit on other women while out with this one.

5. ENTERTAINMENT (en-ter-tayn-ment) n. Female....A good movie, concert, play or book. Male.....Anything that can be done while drinking beer.

6. FLATULENCE (flach-u-lens) n. Female....An embarrassing byproduct of indigestion. Male....A source of entertainment, self-expression, male bonding.

7. MAKING LOVE (may-king luv) n. Female....The greatest expression of intimacy a couple can achieve. Male....Call it whatever you want, just as long as we do it.

8. REMOTE CONTROL (ri-moht kon-trohl) n. Female....A device for changing from one TV channel to another. Male....A device for scanning through all 375 channels every 5 minutes

A woman gets home, screeches her car into the driveway, runs into the house, slams the door and shouts at the top of her lungs, "Honey, pack your bags. I won the lottery!" The husband says, "Oh my God! What should I pack, beach stuff or mountain stuff?" "Doesn't matter," she says, "Just get the hell out!"

LA COMPUTER V. LE COMPUTER

A French-language teacher was explaining to her class that in French, unlike English, nouns are designated as either masculine or feminine. "House" for instance, is feminine-"la maison." "Pencil", however, is masculine-"le crayon." A student asked, "What gender is 'computer'?" Instead of giving the answer, the teacher split the class into two groups, male and female, and asked them to decide for themselves whether "computer" should be a masculine or a feminine noun. Each group was asked to give four reasons for their recommendation. The men's group decided that "computer" should definitely be of the feminine gender ("la computer"), because: 1. no one but their creator understands their internal logic; 2. the native language they use to communicate with other computers is incomprehensible to everyone else; 3. even the smallest mistakes are stored in long term memory for possible later retrieval; and 4. as soon as you make a commitment to one, you find yourself spending half your paycheck on accessories for it. (No chuckling guys...this gets better!!!) The women's group, however, concluded that computers should be Masculine ("le computer"), because: 1. in order to do anything with them, you have to turn them on; 2. they have a lot of data but still can't think for themselves; 3. they are supposed to help you solve problems, but half the time they ARE the problem; and 4. as soon as you commit to one, you realize that if you had waited a little longer, you could have gotten a better model. The women won!

A man went into a local tavern and took a seat at the bar next to a women patron..He turned to her and said, "This is a special day, I'm celebrating." "What a coincidence," said the woman, "I'm celebrating, too". She clinked glasses with him and asked, "What are you celebrating?" "I'm a chicken farmer," he replied. "For years all my hens were infertile, but today they're finally fertile." "What a coincidence," the woman said. "My husband and I have been trying to have a child. Today, my gynecologist told me I'm pregnant! "How did your chickens become fertile?" she asked. "I switched cocks," he replied. "What a coincidence," she said.

EXPENSIVE COSMETICS

Luke's wife bought a new line of expensive cosmetics guaranteed to make her look years younger. After a lengthy sitting before the mirror applying the "miracle" products she asked, "Darling, honestly what age would you say I am?" Looking over her carefully, Luke replied, "Judging from your skin, twenty; your hair, eighteen; and your figure, twenty-five." "Oh, you flatterer!" she gushed. "Hey, wait a minute!" Luke interrupted. "I haven't added them up yet."

A man was walking down the street when he was accosted by a particularly dirty and shabby-looking homeless man who asked him for a couple of dollars for dinner. The man took out his wallet, extracted ten dollars and asked, "If I give you this money, will you buy some beer with it instead?" "No, I had to stop drinking years ago," the homeless man replied. "Will you use it to gamble instead of buying food?" the man asked. "No, I don't gamble," the homeless man said, "I need everything I can get just to stay alive." "Will you spend the money on greens fees at a golf course instead of food?" the man asked. "Are you NUTS!" replied the homeless man. "I haven't played golf in 20 years!" "Will you spend the money on a woman in the red light district instead of food?" the man asked. "What disease would I get for ten lousy bucks?!!" exclaimed the homeless man. "Well," said the man, "I'm not going to give you the money. Instead, I'm going to take you home for a terrific dinner cooked by my wife." The homeless man was astounded. "Won't your wife be furious with you for doing that?" I know I'm dirty, and I probably smell pretty disgusting." The man replied, "That's okay. I just want her to see what a man looks like who's given up beer, gambling, golf, and sex."

SOUND BITES FROM THE ATHEN OLYMPICS

Here are the top nine comments made by sports commentators and participants so far during the Summer Olympics that they would like to take back:

1. Weightlifting commentator: "This is Gregoriava from Bulgaria. I saw her snatch this morning during her warm up and it was amazing."

2. Dressage commentator: "This is really a lovely horse and I speak from personal experience since I once mounted her mother."

3. Gymnast: "I owe a lot to my parents, especially my mother and father."

4. Boxing Analyst: "Sure there have been injuries, and even some deaths in boxing, but none of them really that serious."

5. Softball announcer: "If history repeats itself, I should think we can expect the same thing again."

6. Basketball analyst: "He dribbles a lot and the opposition doesn't like it. In fact you can see it all over their faces."

7. At the rowing medal ceremony: "Ah, isn't that nice, the wife of the IOC president is hugging the cox of the British crew."

8. Soccer commentator: "Julian Dicks is everywhere. It's like they've got eleven Dicks on the field."

9. Tennis commentator: "One of the reasons Andy is playing so well is that, before the final round his wife takes out his balls and kisses them...Oh my God, what have I just said?"

PEARLY GATES

Three men died on Christmas Eve and were met by Saint Peter at the pearly gates. "In honor of this holy season," Saint Peter said, "you must each possess something that symbolizes Christmas to get into heaven!" The first man fumbled through his pockets and pulled out a lighter. He flicked it on. "It represents a candle," he said. "You may pass through the pearly gates," Saint Peter said. The second man reached into his pocket and pulled out a set of keys. He shook them and said, "They're bells". Saint Peter said, "You may pass through the pearly gates." The third man started searching desperately through his pockets and finally pulled out a pair of woman's panties. St. Peter looked at the man with a raised eyebrow and asked, "And just what do those symbolize?" The man replied, "They're Carol's."

TEACHING KIDS THE WORD 'FASCINATE'

A grade school teacher in Kentucky asked her students to use the word "fascinate" in a sentence. Molly put up her hand and said, "My family went to my granddad's farm, and we all saw his pet sheep. It was fascinating." The teacher said, "That was good, but I wanted you to use the word "fascinate, not fascinating". Sally raised her hand. She said, "My family went to see Rock City and I was fascinated." The teacher said "Well, that was good Sally, but I wanted you to use the word "fascinate." Little Johnny raised his hand. The teacher hesitated because she had been burned by Little Johnny before. She finally decided there was no way he could damage the word "fascinate", so she called on him. Johnny said, "My aunt Gina has a sweater with ten buttons, but her boobs are so big she can only fasten eight." The teacher cried.

THE 10 COMMANDMENTS OF MARRIAGE

Commandment 1. Marriages are made in heaven. But then again, so are thunder and lightning.

Commandment 2. If you want your wife to listen and pay strict attention to every word you say, talk in your sleep.

Commandment 3. Marriage is grand – and divorce is at least 100 grand!

Commandment 4. Married life is very frustrating. In the first year of marriage, the man speaks and the woman listens. In the second year, the woman speaks and the man listens. In the third year, they both speak and the neighbors listen.

Commandment 5. When a man opens the door of his car for his wife, you can be sure of one thing: Either the car is new or the wife.

Commandment 6. Marriage is when a man and woman become as one. The trouble starts when they try to decide which one.

Commandment 7. Before marriage, a man will lie awake all night thinking about something you say. After marriage, he will fall asleep before you finish.

Commandment 8. Every man wants a wife who is beautiful, understanding, economical, and a good cook. But the law allows only one wife.

Commandment 9. Marriage and love are purely a matter of chemistry. That is why wives treats husbands like toxic waste.

Commandment 10. A man is incomplete until he is married. After that, he is finished.

A powerful senator dies after a prolonged illness. His soul arrives in heaven and is met by St. Peter at the entrance. "Welcome to Heaven," says St. Peter. "Before you settle in, it seems there is a problem. We seldom see a high official around these parts, you see, so we're not sure what to do with you." "No problem, just let me in," says the guy. "Well, I'd like to but I have orders from higher up. What we'll do is have you spend one day in Hell and one in Heaven. Then you can choose where to spend eternity." "Really, I've made up my mind. I want to be in Heaven," says the senator. "I'm sorry but we have our rules."

And with that, St. Peter escorts him to the elevator and he goes down, down, down to Hell. The doors open and he finds himself in the middle of a green golf course. In the distance is a club and standing in front of it are all his friends and other politicians who had worked with him, everyone is very happy and in evening attire. They run to greet him, hug him, and reminisce about the good times they had while getting rich at the expense of the people. They play a friendly game of golf and then dine on lobster and caviar.

Also present is the Devil, who really is a very friendly guy who has a good time dancing and telling jokes. They are having such a good time that before he realizes it, it is time to go. Everyone gives him a big hug and waves while the elevator rises. The elevator goes up, up, up and the door reopens in Heaven where St. Peter is waiting for him. "Now it's time to visit Heaven." So 24 hours pass with the senator joining a group of contented souls moving from cloud to cloud, playing the harp and singing. They have a good time and, before he realizes it, the 24 hours have gone by and St. Peter returns.

"Well then, you've spent a day in Hell and another in Heaven. Now choose your eternity." He reflects for a minute, then the senator answers, "Well, I would never have said it, I mean Heaven has been delightful, but I think I would be better off in Hell." So St. Peter escorts him to the elevator and he goes down, down, down to Hell.

Now the doors of the elevator open and he is in the middle of a barren land covered with waste and garbage. He sees all his friends, dressed in rags, picking up the trash and putting it in black bags. The Devil comes over to him and lays his arm on his neck. "I don't understand," stammers the senator. "Yesterday I was here and there was a golf course and club and we ate lobster and caviar and danced and had a great time. Now all there is, is a wasteland full of garbage and my friends look miserable. The Devil looks at him, smiles and says, "Yesterday we were campaigning...Today you voted for us!" VOTE WISELY THIS COMING ELECTION!!

Life in the 21st Century

You know you're living in the 21st century when...

1. You accidentally enter your password on the microwave.

2. You haven't played solitaire with real cards in years.

3. You have a list of 15 phone numbers to reach your family of 3.

4. You e-mail the person who works at the desk next to you.

5. Your reason for not staying in touch with friends and family is that they don't have e-mail.

6. Your grandmother asks you to send her a JPEG file of your newborn so she can create a screen saver.

7. You buy a computer and 3 months later it's out of date and sells for half the price, or less than you paid for it.

8. Using real money, instead of a credit or debit card, to make a purchase would be a hassle and take planning.

10. You consider second-day air delivery painfully slow.

11. Your dining room table is now your flat filing cabinet.

12. Your idea of being organized is multiple-colored Post-it notes.

13. You hear of most of your jokes via e-mail instead of in person.

14. You get an extra phone line so you can get phone calls.

15. You disconnect from the Internet and you get this awful feeling, as if you just pulled the plug on a loved one.

16. You wake up at 2 AM to go to the bathroom and check your e-mail on your way back to bed.

17. After a long day at work, you go home and still answer the phone in a business manner.

18. You make phone calls from home, and you automatically dial "9" to get an outside line.

19. You've been sitting at the same desk for four years and have worked for three different companies.

20. You learn about your redundancy on the 11 o'clock news.

21. Your boss doesn't have the ability to do your job.

22. You pull up in your own driveway and use your cell phone to see if anyone is home.

23. Every commercial on television has a website at the bottom of the screen.

24. Leaving the house without your cell phone, which you didn't have the first 20 or 30 (or 40) years of your life, is now a cause for panic. You turn around to go back and get it.

25. You get up in the morning and go online before getting your coffee.

26. You're reading this and nodding and laughing.

27. Even worse, you know exactly to whom you are going to forward this message.

28. You are too busy to notice there was no #9 on this list.

29. You actually scrolled back up to check that there wasn't a #9 on this list.

AND NOW U R LAUGHING---at yourself.

Go on, forward this to your friends...you know you want to!

About the Author

Dr. Alan G. Greene, a retired Radiologist living in Boston, married, with three grown children. Interested in art, music, travel, long walks on the beach (this is starting to sound too much like an ad in the personals).

www.ingramcontent.com/pod-product-compliance
Lightning Source LLC
Chambersburg PA
CBHW021146070326
40689CB00044B/1152